FOLLOWING CHRIST
IN A
CONSUMER SOCIETY

THE SPIRITUALITY OF
CULTURAL RESISTANCE

John Francis Kavanaugh

ORBIS BOOKS

Maryknoll, New York 10545

Seventh Printing, March 1988

The Catholic Foreign Mission Society of America (Maryknoll) recruits and trains people for overseas missionary service. Through Orbis Books Maryknoll aims to foster the international dialogue that is essential to mission. The books published, however, reflect the opinions of their authors and are not meant to represent the official position of the society.

Manuscript Editor: Robert R. Barr

Library of Congress Cataloging in Publication Data

Kavanaugh, John F.
  Following Christ in a consumer society

  Bibliography: p.
  1. Sociology, Christian—United States.
2. Christian life—Catholic authors. I. Title.
BT738.K37   261.8   81-38359
ISBN 0-88344-090-3 (pbk.)   AACR2

To the Communities, the brotherhood, the families; and especially to those who in word and act helped bring this together: Patrick and Jeanne, Michael and Mary Beth, John and Julie; to Mahon, Tom, Jay, Catherine, Virginia, and Ann.

When it comes to the Catholic church, I go to the right as far as I can go. But when it comes to labor, pacifism and civil rights then I go as far as I can to the left.

—*Dorothy Day to Stanley Vishnewski*

CONTENTS

PART TWO
THE PERSONAL FORM

THE SEARCH FOR A PARADOXICAL READERSHIP

I write for two quite disparate groups, who share, if little else, the wholeheartedness of their diverse commitments to either social justice or the life of faith. I am especially writing for those who, while committed to faith or justice, have acknowledged and admitted a need for something to either embody their faith or sustain their passion for equity. In the past few years, I have been privileged by friendships with both kinds of persons. I have seen many priests and nuns committed to work in city ghettos, having lost their sense of faith or prayer, soon lose their passion for the poor. I have talked with married couples clinging to their faith, struggling to ward off a loss of passion for each other and for life. And I continue to dream of bringing together radicalized Christians who seek the support of a profound faith with intensely orthodox believers who seek to give their faith a concrete historical impact. Fideists and activists need each other to be whole. They need each other even to be who they are.

People who have taken social justice seriously are, quite simply, those still working at it. You may be a humanist with unshakable faith that men and women are not expendable. You may be a parish priest who wonders if there is any chance to reveal the ugly truth about racism and inequity to your people in a way that makes sense to you and challenges them to action. You may be a young single or married person laboring with the poor or disenfranchised, working in political organizations or in our schools, and wondering if you can possibly hold on to your commitment while the fire of hope threatens to flicker out. You may be someone who feels betrayed by your own church while you aspire to live the gospel values it taught you.

The first half of this book will make sense to you. But it is the second half that is written for you. Laboring for justice demands the support of a culture-transcending *faith*. And the faith to which you are invited is found in the revelation of Jesus Christ and embodied in the deepest traditions of the Christian Church. I hope that you may discover the truly revolutionary, political, and social implications of Christ's message, of prayer and sacrament, of permanent commitment, and of community life.

The first half of this book, on the other hand, is written for the person who takes faith, especially the Catholic faith, seriously. You may find the second half of the book encouraging or even exhilarating, but the strength of anything it has to say is intimately related to the chapters of the first half, which you may well find irritating or disturbing.

You may be a married couple painfully wondering whether you are all alone in living marital fidelity in this society. You possibly have children whose hearts you feel are being seduced by some alien gospel and empty belief system. You may love the sacraments but wonder what connection they have to life. You may have a desire to know Christ more deeply as the Master of your life, but not quite feel his presence in your lived struggles. You may question what your faith calls you to in a culture of institutional abortion, pornography, and the decline of family life. You may be seeking methods to resist the injustices of the world, but not know where to turn.

The suggestion that this book offers to you is this: authentic faith is constituted by justice, expressed and embodied in our social relations as well as in our personal lives. The issues which bother you are *economic and political* problems, as well as moral and religious. And problems which may not bother you— armament, capital punishment, racism, and the like—are religious and spiritual problems as well as political ones. Although justice is not all there is to faith, when you are truly living your faith you are doing justice. And when you are doing true justice you are living your faith.

The danger in having such a strangely dual audience is that both groups could be either missed or alienated. The message I hope to communicate, moreover, can be lost in the perplexing confusion about faith and justice issues that is presently haunting our culture.

The rise of the "new conservatism" is a case in point. As I see this movement, often associated with morality and a form of Christian faith, it is not a conserving of what is richest and deepest in human beings, but a preserving of ourselves from the facts. It is a conservatism not of principle, but of pragmatism. It hungers for the legitimations of power and prestige—especially economic, military, and ideological. And it represses all suggestions that right order has yet to be achieved in our country. It is a conservatism of self-interest.

This new conservatism is the fruit of two complementary but dangerous tendencies: the tendency to *separate* faith from the work of justice (active love and service) and the tendency to *equate* faith with a particular form of social, political, or national power.

The danger of the first tendency is that it fails to recognize that society and culture are intimately interwoven with spirituality and faith. The power of religious aspiration is rendered innocuous and ineffective when it is separated from the concrete demands of justice and love for others. Both the established "secular" and "religious" worlds feed this debilitating separation—not of church from state, but of faith from lived social reality.

Newsy journals chide bishops for trying to legislate morality in their protesting of abortion. Women missionaries who were brutally killed in Central America are passed off by some right-wing pundits as do-gooders who had no business working for the poor and oppressed. Social commentators taunt people of faith who take stands concerning world hunger, prisons, and the inequitable distribution of wealth. Church leaders are subjected to State Department pressure when they resist propaganda on arms spending, on military aid to El Salvador, on cutbacks in federal assistance to the poor.

On the other hand, when some clerics, religious, or lay persons try to speak to their own church people about justice, racism, capital punishment, or militarism, they are frequently told, "Don't bring politics into the pulpit. Talk to us of religion." It is not unthinkable that Mary, the mother of Jesus, would be unable to speak her Magnificat from our church sanctuaries, smacking as it does of poverty-talk, justice, and casting the mighty down from their thrones. And so, the "people of God" join forces with *Time* and *Newsweek* in their prying apart of politics and spirituality, in their sundering of faith from justice.

It is a most dangerous separation. For it is precisely this splitting of faith from social reality that seduces the religious impulse into a stance of mere accommodation to political and economic power. Hence, the second dangerous tendency: the *identification* of faith with cultural standards, even cultural idols.

Recent events provide compelling examples of the ways that Christians are more committed in *lived* faith to the gospels of nation and culture than to the gospel of Jesus. When Pope John Paul II came to the United States, Roman Catholic commentators of the right and left went to great pains to explain to television audiences that the pope did not fully understand the "facts" of American Life—whether economic, military, or sexual. The actual problem is, however, that North Americans are not sufficiently critical of their own patterns of life—especially with respect to sex, war, and money. The pope was calling for an evangelical generosity in *all* areas—based upon the radical dignity of the human person revealed in the gospel of Christ. The pope also saw the intrinsic relatedness among all these areas, in the light of faith, and how they are influenced by cultural ideology rather than human sensibility. This relatedness, however, was ignored or repressed. For to confront it would mean to change our own attitudes and behaviors toward nationalism, poverty, and justice.

A second phenomenon is the fact that many of those who do claim to see the relationship between Jesus and politics have reduced Christ to Americanism and capitalism. Some of them, assuming the terminology of "morality" and "majority," continually associate Christianity with military ascendency, financial success, and vindictiveness against criminals or marginal people. They come close to extinguishing the fire and compassion of Jesus' own message and life. On many Sunday morning media presentations of Christianity, we hear much of money and success, often of psychological stability and social popularity, frequently of the glories of capitalism and the dangers of socialism, but rarely of the poor, the suffering, the rejected, and disenfranchised; rarely of the Christ who was crucified, unsuccessful, imprisoned, and abandoned. Such is the impoverishment of a faith intimidated and consumed by cultural imperatives.

The impoverishment and domestication of the Christian faith, consequently, is not only the central problem of my search for a paradoxical readership; it is also the central problem addressed by this book. I intend to show the intrinsic and necessary relationship between a living faith and an activist love. At the same time I will suggest how it is that men and women of faith can so easily be led into a position of submission before national, economic, and cultural idols.

I propose to activists that they become more profoundly rooted in faith: in the life and action of Jesus and in the life of a believing people.

I propose to people who profess a serious belief in Jesus that they become more deeply activist in their loving service and more fully critical of the ways their faith has become acculturated.

In answer to the problem of a faith ineffectually isolated from justice, this book offers neither more interiority nor more activism, but precisely an integration of both: an activism that is truly revolutionary and a faith that is fully holy: saintly revolution.

In answer to the problem of faith being co-opted by culture, this book suggests how the life of Jesus, how his saving action, how his people and its traditions, all offer a most stunning contrast to cultural idols. We must be willing to disengage our commitment in Christ from the illusions of nationalistic myth, military might, and economic supremacy. We must be courageous enough to undertake a life of resistance.

The problem of finding people who might respond to the whole of this book, consequently, is very much like the difficulty we face in confronting both Christ and culture in an integral manner. It is a risk, but it is worth it. And there are hopeful signs in the churches that the convergence of justice and spirituality is upon us. If persons of traditional Catholic faith are repelled by the social critique of America or the mention of Marx, at least they might be invited more deeply into the faith which calls them to justice and compassion for the poor, if they take that faith seriously. If social activists, disillusioned with the broken promises and inconsistencies of a sinful church, will not take seriously the talk of sacraments and prayer, perhaps at least they will be led into a deeper recognition of the imposing reality which confronts them. It may be hoped that they will see how high the stakes are, how great the need is for some sustaining hope or faith or person to live and die for.

Part One is a critique of American society under the controlling concept of the "Commodity Form." When we perceive ourselves and others as things, when we live and behave under the "form" or in the image of the commodity, we invariably produce lives of violence, fear, manipulation, and alienation. This critique is framed by a discussion of some insights which Karl Marx could offer for a Christian critique of society and a schematic presentation of a Christian anthropology. The purpose of Part One is to reveal the spiritual crisis at the heart of social and political and economic evils. Our problem is idolatry. Its presence is systemic.

Part Two is a presentation of the "Personal Form" of perceiving, valuing, and living as revealed in the person of Christ. Its purpose is to reveal the societal and political implications of believing in Jesus Christ, and to suggest the ways of sustaining a Christian-activist life through sacramentality, prayer, commitment, family, and community. The way of Christ is the way of freedom. It, too, is systemic. His claim upon our lives is total; and it is in collision with our culture.

The entire book is largely interpretative—an attempt to see behind the veil of appearances in our culture and penetrate to the meaning of a religion so often supposedly fought for but rarely lived. Although I offer an annotated bibliography as appendix, I do not attempt in the text to document facts or observations. Rather, I ask you to direct your energy and attention to the lines of interpretation. Since, moreover, this is not a book of fundamental or philosophical ethics, no specific arguments are given to support my own positions against war, abortion, armament, sexual hedonism, or unrestrained capitalism. My purpose is not so much to establish the foundations of particular moral positions as it is to unveil the connections between them. I would rather reveal the relationship between death row and abortion factories than prove the inhumanity of either. I would rather suggest the collaboration of hedonism with the dissolution of marriage and with the free market than insist upon or demonstrate the evil of each.

Just as my ethical convictions are not established here but are offered as personal rational choices, so also my appeal to Jesus Christ is not "justified" by any apologetic or dogmatic argument. It is, as it stands, quite simply an appeal and belief that I invite others to share in commitment. I write as a social and political communitarian, an evangelical Roman Catholic, whose final trust rests on the love of God made manifest to humanity in Jesus Christ.

FOLLOWING CHRIST
IN A
CONSUMER SOCIETY

PART ONE
THE COMMODITY
FORM

CHAPTER ONE

THE CHRISTIAN-MARXIST MATRIX

It has become fashionable in our time to describe the human search for truth as a journey involving "many paths to a single mountain top." The phrase suggests a common ground of our longings and struggles. It hints at some persisting universal goal worthy of our striving. And it implies that, within this common striving, all our various, individual, idiosyncratic ways up the mountain are equally valid and valuable.

But what if we struggle up two different mountains, one whose apex enthrones the thing, the other exalting the human person? Or what if, on the single mountain, some paths lead only to a precipice? Or what if, as we travel, one specific path emerges as the surest and the loveliest, the most fruitful, the most freeing? Perhaps it does matter which path we choose to follow. Perhaps the latent relativism of the phrase, "many paths to the mountain top," is a trap we should be wary of.

None the less, the "path" metaphor has the advantage of suggesting a personal journey toward truth. I intend in this book to lay aside the rigor of scientific investigations and philosophic methods. Those disciplines can be left for a better time and better hands. What I hope to describe through these pages is a path which seems to me the clear, sure way to the top of the mountain.

It is not a path entirely of my own making. I must admit to the powerful attraction and influence of Catholicism upon me. I must also admit that the ghost of Karl Marx haunts some of my footsteps on this path. Marx's presence is especially noteworthy since that name often conjures up visions of "purges," "atheistic materialism," "totalitarianism," "economic determinism," and all manner of other generally evil spectors. (Catholicism may well conjure up similar images, except that its materialism and determinism would be quite relentlessly theistic.)

Such images are the price I pay for having a history at the foundation of the path I am tracing. But the fact that I value much of Marx and more of Catholicism does not compel me to defend all of either. It is what I apprehend at the heart of both that commands my attention and allegiance: the cherishing and exalting of humanity.

The convergence of Catholicism with the thought of Marx can certainly be seen, it seems to me, in the recent efforts of the theologians of liberation in South and Central America. My own experience of such a convergence, however, comes not from a Third World perspective, but from the consciousness of a Catholic living under advanced industrialized technocracy. It corresponds to the combination of themes found in the writings and speeches of Pope John Paul II: the experience of human alienation in consumerist capitalist economic systems (paralleling the same dynamic in totalitarian statist regimes) and the discovery of human emancipation in the person of Jesus Christ. In fact, the central sections of the encyclical *Redemptor Hominis* are remarkably persuasive expressions of the convergence of a humanism not at all alien to Marx and a powerfully transcendent faith in Christ.

When I read the New Testament in faith and in community, I apprehend Jesus Christ as the fullest revelation of what it means to be God and what it means to be a human person. He is the meeting point between the human and the divine. This union is brought about not by a rejection of his humanity nor by a domination of or escape from it, but a full yielding to its poverty and promise. In Christ's total acceptance of his humanness, he is utterly open to and one with humanity's source and purpose. For it is God, our beginning and our end, who quickens our highest instincts as men and women, from whom we are called forth into time, and to whom we are drawn in our longings. As Christ reveals the God who would wipe away every human tear—even if it would mean becoming one with those tears—he also reveals the utter irreplaceability of each human person even in his or her struggles and dyings. But much more must be said of this later.

The driving motive of Marx's life was that men and women might recover the humanity which had been ripped from them in the very act of creating and producing their own handiwork. Marx was filled with outrage that things had come to replace persons in value. He saw humans as investing their whole reality and purpose in what is a mere fragment of themselves: the commodity.

> The commodity appears, at first sight, a very trivial thing, and easily understood. Its analysis shows that it is, in reality, a very queer thing, abounding in metaphysical subtleties and theological niceties. . . .
>
> There is a definite social relation between men that assumes, in their eyes, the fantastic form of a relation between things. In order, therefore, to find an analogy, we must have recourse to the mist-enveloped regions of the religious world. In that world the productions of the human brain appear as independent beings endowed with life and entering into relation both with one another and the human race. So it is in the world of commodities with the products of men's hands. This I call the Fetishism which attaches itself to the products of labor. . . .
>
> The relations connecting the labor of one individual with that of the rest appear not as the direct social relations between individuals at work, but as what they really are: material relations between persons and social relations between things.

Thus in the early pages of *Das Kapital* does Karl Marx (supposedly at the most "coldly deterministic" stage of his life) complain that material relations between things have displaced truly human and social relations between persons. He compares our relationship to commodities with his notion of religion, wherein humans subject themselves to the imagined products of their thoughts. Thus he sees the commodity functioning as a god or, more specifically, a "fetish": relating to a mere part of the beloved as if it were the entire beloved. The commodity, like a god, achieves an independent existence over and against men and women. We begin to worship things, to relate to them as if they were persons; and we relate to other persons as if they were things.

Such is Marx's quarrel with the world throughout his life. As a young man in 1844, he wrote of the need for love, creativity, and human freedom in an inverted world where money, profit, and production reigned as supreme values. In his middle-life work, he claimed that the true basis of values, wealth, and human purpose was not the realm of the thing, but the unfolding of human aspirations and potentiality in creative activity. Finally, his titanic and often misunderstood *Capital* is shot through with moral outrage at the degradation of human life and rings with a profound commitment to the dignity of the human person. I find Marx's writings utterly impossible to understand without a continual focus on his ethical passion and on his implicit but nonetheless crucial need for a philosophy of the human person. Because such a philosophy and ethics were both crucial and merely implicit, the intention of Marx has been wildly misunderstood, and at a terrifying human cost. His devotion to human emancipation and the philosophical justification for such a devotion never having been elaborated, Marx's name became easily linked with crude philosophical materialism and political oppression.

Nonetheless, he is a companion on the path I travel—not only for his sense of justice and prophetic indictment of social evil, but also because he provides me with a sense of socio-cultural-economic critique in the name of human dignity. While appearing at first hostile to faith, Marx, like Aristotle in metaphysics, may be, in the area of society and history, a support of faith. More specifically, Marx provides me with four important reflective themes (not exclusively his own) to employ in examining the gospel of capitalism.

THE DIALECTICAL TOTALITY

Within a culture or a social system, within any human grouping, enterprise, or relationship, within experience itself, all of the "parts" are intimately related to each other and to the "whole." No isolated fragment or part can be fully understood and evaluated outside of its relatedness to the other parts and to the totality. An exclusive concentration on one aspect of experience, for example, leads to a one-sided interpretation of the world and consequent truncated forms of behavior. Thus if I solely emphasize the "feeling" dimensions of experience, I will have a severely restricted view of other people and be seriously limited in my range of behavior toward them. I will become dominated by the partiality of feeling. The same can be said for exclusively focusing on rationality or sensation.

On a more familiar level, if a family is to grow and function healthily, its life and purpose cannot be dominated by only one member or part of the family. It is precisely in the members' interrelatedness to each other and to the family-as-total-group that development, freedom, and love can take place for each and all. This emphasis upon relatedness by no means excludes all attempts to focus on and reflect on any one member's problems or contributions. Such focusing and analysis help us understand the relationships and dynamics of the family as a totality. We must, however, always begin and end with a synthesis, a "dialectically related whole" which is not reducible to any one of the members or "parts."

Applying this insight to Marx's theories, we find that he held our social and cultural "totality" to be the ongoing labor of men and women in history—the creative and free expression of our humanness through artistic, theoretical, and technological production. All of the parts of our human world influence one another, but Marx was at special pains to point out that this interrelatedness had been forgotten. He insisted that religious, political, or philosophical movements could not be adequately understood or challenged apart from the economic ambient in which they flourished. He maintained, moreover, that we are blinded to the ways in which the economic system is supported by other "realms," such as education, political structures, and philosophical worldviews. He also attempted to show how one particular economic system—industrial capitalism—had succeeded in blinding people to the fact that they were serving the life of the system rather than having the system serve them. Thus the totality (the human world) was being dominated by a partiality (the capitalistic manner of production).

At the same time, it seems to me that Marx failed to reintegrate the elements in his analysis. In his effort to show the economic determinisms of society, he came dangerously close to compressing the entire human world into the economic "piece" which he so wholeheartedly investigated. Thus in Marx's own theory, the "part" (economics) seems to dominate the "whole" (human reality). And it is this lapse which leads Marx into persistent difficulties in grounding both human freedom and human dignity.

As a Christian trying to understand my relationship to society, I can be assisted by Marx's notion of "totality" as well as by his mistake. Is the separation of faith from justice a misunderstanding of the totality of our lives? Does such a separation lead to a domination by one "part?" Do we have to choose between faith and justice?

If we do, we lose the power of their interrelatedness. The church loses the integrity of Christ's message (loving one's self, one's neighbor, and God), people leave the community thinking they have to choose between God and humanity, the faith of activists disappears with their activism often following, and the action of believers becomes timid and disconnected. On the other hand, activists emphasizing only the justice part have lost their strongest support for being just and for calling others to justice, just as the pietist emphasizing faith alone finds that the fruit of faith—loving action—inevitably disappears.

If, however, we remain faithful to the totality of our lives, we see that the issue of Christian faith is love. We are also able to ask questions such as those that follow which might otherwise evade us. Could it be that there are *economic* conditions that *foster* the breaking of the ten commandments? Does a given economic or social system inhibit personal commitment, prayer, or the sharing of our goods? Is there a cultural bias against the living of lifelong vows? Does chastity have a political impact? Is marital fidelity a social force for justice? In answering such questions, we might more fully realize that there is nothing in the realm of the social, the political, or the economic which does not influence or is not influenced by the realm of Spirit. And there is nothing in the realm of Spirit which does not influence or is not influenced by history.

TOTALIZING CRITIQUE

In 1843, Marx committed himself to a "relentless criticism of all existing conditions." All of his subsequent writings, many titled or subtitled "critique," doggedly implemented that commitment. He tried to make his critiques "total," calling into question *all* prevailing modes of perception, especially the economic, in the name of humanity. He relentlessly pointed out that most philosophical and economic worldviews contained a hidden premise which itself had to be subjected to questioning and criticism: the premise that men and women had no right to their own labor, that they were subservient to the market, that they were somehow slaves to their own products.

This is quite similar to the critique offered by Pope John Paul II in *Redemptor Hominis*:

Man cannot relinquish himself or the place in the visible world that belongs to him; he cannot become the slave of things, the slave of economic systems, the slave of production, the slave of his own products. . . . It is a matter of the *whole* of the dynamism of life and civilization. It is a matter of the meaningfulness of the various initiatives of everyday life and also of the premises for many civilization programs, political programs, economic ones, social ones, state ones and many others (No. 16).

Today a totalizing critique should unveil the presuppositions and values which link partialized issues like racism, male or female chauvinism, hedonism, revolutionary terrorism, euthanasia, and economic oppression. Without such a critique, those issues seem unrelated and isolated. They can be attacked only on their own limited terms. Any such attack will be fragmentary and therefore ineffectual. The root problems, the root causes, the "premises underlying the whole dynamic of life and civilization," will persist—unnamed, unexamined, unassailable. This lack of totalizing critique allows one to simultaneously espouse the ridiculously antithetical positions of soft, liberal pacifism toward Indochina, fiercely militant support of Israel, and benign, bored indifference to New York's abortion mills.

Such diverse issues as excessive consumption, moral relativism, competition, the dissolution of family life, and the devaluation of the human person are all bound together into a total system of perceiving, valuing, and behaving which I call the Commodity Form. The preeminence of the commodity and its effect on our consciousness and purpose provides the crucial link between widely divergent moral and social struggles. The Commodity Form sustains and legitimates the entire fabric of dehumanization. So it is the Commodity Form which must be unveiled, which must be subjected to totalizing critique.

A totalizing critique which is also dialectical will show how the Commodity Form of life interpenetrates the various arenas of our experience and thought. The Commodity Form intensifies the unfocusing of the individual, the loss of interiority, and the fragmentation of personal identity. It is also a social force which fragments the community of persons, setting each against each and the individual against all. We experience it, consequently, as much in our alienation from one another as in our alienation from our selves. The Commodity Form touches our experience through the style of life we are expected to assume: consumerism, competition, hoarding, planned obsolescence, and unnecessary waste. It frames all discussion of the wide-ranging justice issues which confound us in their diversity and expanse. And it offers the major cultural mode of pretense: flight from our own poverty and that of men and women around us.

A full-fledged critique will illuminate the multifarious expressions of the Commodity Form of life. And, once we discover the range and depth of its impact upon our lives, we can envision an equally extensive and integrated life of resistance to its hold over our behaviors, our consciousness, our feeling and emotions.

But critique by itself is a notoriously inadequate response to human struggles. Marx himself grew increasingly vague in formulating a positive view of humanity which might replace Capitalism. That vagueness sprang partly from the difficulty of predicting how a future classless society might look; but it also issued from Marx's own feeble philosophy of human nature. The energy of total critique concerning the Commodity Form consequently must be complemented by the positive moment of elaborating its alternative: the Personal Form. This will be the project of the second half of this book.

IDOLATRY

Psalm 115 could have been written by Marx (or perhaps was indirectly instrumental in much of what Marx actually did write):

> Their idols are silver and gold,
> made by the hands of men.
> They have mouths that cannot speak,
> and eyes that cannot see;
> they have ears that cannot hear,
> nostrils that cannot smell;
> with their hands they cannot feel,
> with their feet they cannot walk,
> and no sound comes from their throats.
> Their makers grow to be like them,
> and so do all who trust in them. . . .

What Marx called the "fetishism of commodities" is simply a form of idolatry in which human persons worship the products of their own hands. Money, Moloch, the Tyranny of Production strip us of our humanity. Living only to labor and to cling to the products of our labor, we recreate ourselves in the image and likeness of our products. We alienate ourselves from each other in competition and in the struggle for possession and profit. We become alienated from our own humanness. Taking upon ourselves the form and reality of things, we lose our most basic senses of intimacy and touch. We can no longer speak our being or perceive our personhood. Human relationships, activities, qualities, become thing-like relations, actions, and qualities.

We become transformed *into* the idols we *trust*. What was even more troublesome to Marx was that we cannot see the ways in which our humanity has been dispossessed. The idol becomes for us a "veil of illusion," preventing us from seeing any other alternative ways of being or living. Marx's *Capital* is actually an attack upon the economic veil of illusion which prevents a true revelation of laboring men and women from taking place. It is an attempt to show once more that the products of human effort are created to serve human needs. In worshipping those products, in living for them, in measuring ourselves by their qualities, we have created a false god which exacts from us our very freedom and personhood.

Idolatry in all of its forms displaces proper human relationships and turns upside down the ordered human world. Idolatry victimizes any person whose life and purpose become reduced to serving a state, technology, ideology, or church. The struggle against idolatry, which Marx's thought exemplifies, is an effort to cast off the distortions which an idolatrous world too often perpetrates, so that political, religious, philosophical, and economic structures may serve humanity rather than hold humans in bondage.

MORAL OUTRAGE

Embarrassing as it was to Lenin and embarrassing as it remains to some contemporary Marxists, the entire span of Karl Marx's work is charged with a sense of moral passion. Marx relentlessly appeals to an underlying conviction that persons cannot be treated as things, that oppression and injustice violate human dignity, that all human expression cries out for autonomy and creative self-realization. This conviction makes *possible* and legitimates the development of Marx's later work as well as the power of his early manuscripts. Marx may never have grounded his conviction philosophically, but he never functioned apart from it. It is his constant assumption and over-arching presupposition.

To this day, however, questions remain, haunting the philosophy of Marxism as profoundly as they belie the historical practice of communist states. What is the proper foundation of and justification for moral outrage? Why does any human action or any social system merit moral indignation? Why is it reprehensible that Marx's proletariat had been impoverished? Why is capitalism bad? Why ultimately should it have worried Marx that men and women were exploited? Answers must be attempted, Lenin's suppression of the questions notwithstanding. They have certainly not been forthcoming from orthodox communist philosophy.

Anglo-American thought has not done much better. And in many cases even the sense of moral passion has been extinguished by a systematic relativizing of moral judgments and a still persistent emotivist theory of ethics. Such a relativism and emotivism in moral theory only serves to legitimate any power structure that presently exists. Moral struggles are termed "emotional issues," incapable of rational or just solution, so what "is" remains the same. The regimenting of power and the numerology of polls determine morality quantitatively. Straightforward moral conviction is unseemly and quaint. Thus the need for unashamed outrage is all the greater.

Yet again, as with critique, outrage is not enough. Some positively articulated understanding of human dignity must be established, either in a philosophical anthropology or in a revelation of the human person's worth and purpose. The absence of such a philosophical foundation and of the moral principles which would necessarily follow has led, and can only lead, to the expendability of millions of persons. The graves of White Russians, the terror bombing of Dresden, Hiroshima, the ovens of Dachau and Auschwitz, the Gulag Archipelago, the Christmas bombing of North Vietnam, the millions of aborted human fetuses, the thousands on death row, testify so.

In my own reflections, the critical and moral passion of Marx and the inspiration of his methodology will be joined to an exposition of Jesus Christ's positive revelation of humanity to itself.

If Marx and Jesus were mutually exclusive as friends and traveling companions, I would unhesitatingly choose Jesus. Marx, even at the moments of his most transcending vision of human promise, does not even begin to approach the revolutionary revelation of freedom and dignity that can be found in the person of Jesus. But I do not see Marx and Jesus as mutually exclusive. If anything, Marx's dream is wholly unrealizable without the Passion—in both senses of the word—of Jesus. The work of liberation theologians, incomplete and rough-hewn as it is, argues the case with increasing cogency. And Pope John Paul's warning, to both East and West, that the human person may never be reduced to a mere means of production alienated from ourselves and from our destiny in Jesus, makes convergence a historical actuality. Marxism and Christianity can be complementary, mutually sustaining forces on our journey—Marx providing some concrete historically critical tools, and Christ revealing the ultimate foundation and fulfillment of our hope.

CHAPTER TWO

BEHIND BELIEF AND THE CULTURAL GOSPEL

GOSPEL AS "FORM" OF LIFE AND PERCEPTION

A "gospel" is a book of revelation, an ultimate source or reference wherein we find ourselves revealed. A gospel is a response to the questions of who we are, what we may hope for, how we may aspire to act, what endures, what is important, what is of true value. A gospel, then, is an expression of who or what is our functional god.

No longer are people so much concerned with the issue of atheism. We used to hear questions like, "Do you believe in God?" But today it is no longer a significant question (if it ever was one). The question more crucially before us is, "What god do you believe in?" The myth of the "value-free" science, much less any other human enterprise, is dead. Everyone, any scientist, any philosopher, any politician, economist, or blue collar worker, has a functional god or some ultimate basis of value. It is not a question of *whether* to believe, *whether* to value, but *what* to believe and value. In other words, once our pretenses of neutrality are given up, where do we really find ourselves and our destinies revealed? What is our book of revelation? What is our gospel?

We will inevitably be confronted with at least two competing gospels or books of revelation in American society. These gospels differ as radically as light and darkness, life and death, freedom and slavery, fidelity and unfaithfulness. They serve as ultimate and competing "forms" of perception, through which we filter all of our experience. Each form, moreover, provides a controlling image for our consciousness in apprehending our selves and our world. These competing life-forms can be expressed as the "gospels" of Personhood and Commodity: the Personal Form and the Commodity Form; the Person-god and the Thing-god. Each has its own "church," you might say, its own cults and liturgical rites, its own special language, and its own concept of the heretical.

One form of life, one gospel, reveals men and women as replaceable and marketable commodities; another gospel, inalterably opposed to the first, reveals persons as irreplaceable and uniquely free beings. Some people having formal membership in a Christian church may in reality follow the gospel of the culture, and belong to the secular church of "the thing." Others, not formally belonging to a Christian church or to a synagogue, may actually be giving their life-commitments to the message and truth revealed in the covenantal Lord of the Jewish Bible or in Jesus Christ as true God and true human person.

CULTURE AS HUMAN:
AMERICAN CULTURE AS GRACED

Setting up such an opposition has, of course, its dangers, oversimplification not being the least of them. A culture is a human creation, with human possibilities for pathology as well as for grace and health. A culture, presumably, is as redeemable as a person. At least we might accept such a possibility as an open question. But I wish to focus upon our own culture as the embodiment of immanently reinforced and legitimated values which permeate our institutions, sustain the accepted "wisdom" of the day, and underwrite our notions of "what really counts," of "what talks." It is in this sense that I will speak of the American culture as a pathological phenomenon which assumes for us an objective reality of its own, and against which we judge ourselves, evaluate our worth, seek our fulfillment, and find our meaning and purpose.

I will be emphasizing the negative aspects of our cultural values, well aware that we have no corner on the market of unfreedom, repression, and injustice. Our culture is not the first, nor is it the worst to have discovered evil. But it is the only one we live in, the one we are most in need of subjecting to critique.

It is true that the American society is graced in countless ways. We nurture a promise of what millions see and experience as a good and free life. We have a marvelously fertile land and an accomplished technology. Our people have often overcome massive internal opposition in attempting to deal equitably with racism, poverty, the needs of other nations, and institutionalized dishonesty at the highest levels of government. We sustain perduring democratic impulse toward equality, fairness, and the checking of our darker impulses. We are privileged with a press which is for the most part free, despite corporate controls and its dependency upon advertising. Americans by their labor and legislation have achieved almost full literacy, health, food and retirement programs, and a force of productive workers invested with self-respect, political power, and considerable security.

But these very "graced" accomplishments, these gifts themselves, are in danger of extinction. American society (and religious faith, including Christianity, to the extent that it has identified with this culture) is in great peril. Human commitment, true personal productivity which serves the human interest, our institutions of family community and citizenship, our sense of justice and respect for freedom, the valuing of life and affection, are all under massive attack.

CULTURE AS INHUMAN:
AMERICAN CULTURE AS DISGRACED

Our severity in judging our value system should not be mitigated by pointing to the failures of other eras or countries in the hope of softening our self-critique. It is none other than *ourselves* whom we must reflect upon, and, if necessary, seek to have changed. We do no service to the truth, much less to the country we profess to love, if we insist that the frequent appearance of evil in other countries and ages somehow absolves us of the evils strangling us. The failures of post-revolutionary France, of Leninist Russia, or of contemporary dictatorships, should serve only to warn us rather than justify their reduplication in our own lives. The fact that I may love my family and even prefer it to all others does not mean that I shouldn't challenge or change it, especially if it is in danger.

It is only at great cost to ourselves and our integrity that we ignore the one million dead in Southeast Asia who have purportedly brought us "peace with honor." The dead do not experience it that way, nor do the one hundred million killed since 1900 in the name of an always "final" but disappearing peace.

It can only be foolishness, not patriotism, to ignore the realities of the present. We *already* live in a country in which the old of our society are victims of what Claire Townsend calls the "last segregation." We already know that some New York insurance companies will pay willingly for the termination of pregnancies but not for deliveries. It is already the case that women from Bedford Stuyvesant, illiterate but hoping to give birth, are directed to abortion-referral lines when they are seeking pre-natal counseling. It has already happened that bureaucratic expertise has seen fit to sterilize young black women without their knowledge.

We already live in a country represented by people who seem to think that the food problem of the world can be solved solely by contraceptives rather than by a more equitable distribution of wealth. We inhabit a country in which there is medical experimentation upon syphilitic prisoners and living aborted fetuses, in which euthanasia laws have been introduced into state legislatures, in which the highest court of the land has institutionalized abortion by reducing the issue of fetal human life to a matter of property and privacy. State executions, nuclear escalations, pregnancy terminations, and disposal of the brain-damaged are arbitrated in terms of cost-benefit analysis.

We already live in a country which feeds its dogs a better diet than a fourth of the world's humans are fed—a phenomenon made painfully clear in our latest marketing discovery of diet-food products for our hapless overweight dogs. We consume more products to take off weight than some countries spend to put it on. We have doubled our meat consumption in the last twenty years and increased the death-related health hazards caused by dietary superfluity. Meanwhile, there is much earnest talk of "lifeboat ethics" and the abandonment of the world's poor because there is "not enough to go around"; and at the same time we continue to suffocate in our pollution-generating abundance.

We already live in a country which has prosecuted illegal wars in secrecy, which has seen fit to execute the greatest saturation terror-bombing in history, which has lionized leaders who have shown little more than contempt for people of the Third World, and which has manipulated, controlled, and ended entire governments of other countries.

Our most recent social, economic, and political byword is "toughness." A leading conservative columnist, often noted for his humane sensibilities, now approves of state murder. Without batting an eye he extols the fact that our economic system is run on envy. Opinion polls indicate the range of our new toughness on human life. Two-thirds of us are for more armament, 63 percent for abortion, and 68 percent for capital punishment. Our toughness in defense is a devastation for the poor—not only in the rest of the world, but in our own cities and communities. Even before the Reagan proposal of a $222 billion military budget for 1982 (the largest peacetime increase in the history of the Pentagon), the amount that the U.S. appropriated for food stamps in fiscal year 1981 would run the Pentagon for a mere 33 minutes. And yet, we are told, it is the poor who must cut back. Our U.S. Food for Peace appropriations would run the Pentagon for three minutes. In fact, *all* of the U.S. contributions to United Nations programs from 1946 to 1978 would run the Pentagon for barely nineteen days.

Finally, we have the luxury of spending almost 50 billion dollars a year on an industry that is in countless ways a nationally institutionalized deception—a fostering of false needs and the creation of false promises. Our world of advertising, the "life-blood" of our economy, tells us from our earliest years that we are despicable and inadequate because of the products we lack. "Datsun saves and sets you free." "Buick is something to believe in." "Coke is the real thing." "Love is Musk." "Don't thank me, thank Listerine."

This is the culture that is already with us, that we breathe. This, I've been told by my students, is "the real world, Father." "Power talks, money talks." These are the self-revelations of a culture and its Gospel. And it is this culture which must be open to critique.

THE HIDDEN UNITY BEHIND THE APPEARANCES

In a totalizing critique, we must ask ourselves what is behind this buzzing phantasmagoria of partialities and disparate problems, only select issues of which we might find equally disturbing or distasteful. What might be the common "form" or perception or pattern of life in all of these observations? What connections might be made? Is there any relationship between our clean bombs, our defense delivery systems, and our antiseptic delivery rooms? Is there any connection between street violence and the women with staples in their navels who populate the pages of our voyeuristic magazines? Is there any relationship between *triage* ("They would be better off dead than living the way they do in India"), the extinction of the brain-damaged, the extermination of the unwanted, and the claim "I had to destroy that village in order to save it"?

It is the totality of the Commodity Form to which we will now turn, to find the matrix of values which underwrites the assault upon everything that is human and graced in our culture.

CHAPTER THREE

THE COMMODITY FORM: CONSUMING AND MARKETING

The pre-eminent values within the Commodity Form of life are marketability and consumption. These two values are the ethical lenses through which we are conditioned to perceive our worth and importance. They have profoundly affected not only our self-understanding but also our modelling of human behavior (into manipulation and aggression), human knowledge (into quantification, observation, and measurement), and human affectivity (into noncommittalness and mechanized sexuality).

A few years ago the Associated Press ran a story about a Dr. Darold Treffert of the Winnebago Mental Health Institute in Wisconsin and his theory that teen-agers were being victimized by what he called "The American Fairy Tale." The story read in part:

> Amy, 15, had always gotten straight "A's" in school, and her parents were extremely upset when she got a B on her report card. "If I fail in what I do," Amy told her parents, "I fail in what I am." The message was part of Amy's suicide note.

"The American Fairy Tale," Treffert claimed, "begins with two themes: that more possessions mean more happiness, that a person who does or produces more is more important."

21

These themes are also the foundational motifs of the Commodity Form. In the family where love must be earned, competed for, won, or proved; in education where value is exclusively rated in terms of production, quantified grades, and competitive standings; in religion with communion counts and Madison Avenue vocation promotions; in the job sweepstakes or in retirement of the expendable: in all these areas, marketability is king. "Will it play in Peoria" is not only the standard of the marketed dishonesty found in the Watergate travesty and its daily declared "inoperative truths"; it has become the criterion of selfhood. Will *I* sell? Will they buy *me*? Diplomas, skills, talents, and roles are mustered from our earliest ages as guarantees against the planned obsolescence characteristic of our products and our persons. If you are unproductive you are unuseful, worthless. You are unwanted, whether you be one of the economically poor, a starving Bengali, a death-row criminal, or a bothersome five-month fetus. The crises that children face in their terror at being replaced is the first premonition of that demeaned life to which so many of our elder retired succumb in their feelings of being worthless and discarded once their marketing days are over.

What this means in effect is that there is no intrinsic human uniqueness or irreplaceable value. The person *is* only insofar as he or she is marketable or productive. Human products, which should be valued only insofar as they enhance and express human worth, become the very standards against which human worth itself is measured. If our life's meaning is dictated by mercantilism and production, then our purpose and value are defined essentially in relation to what we can buy, what we can sell, or—at the very least—what we can hold on to. The uniqueness of an individual's way of being, of the unrepeatable personal qualities in knowing and loving, of relating to life in such a way that can never be duplicated by another person, much less by a thing—these human qualities inevitably disappear in a universe whose ultimates are productivity and marketing.

The form of the commodity which legitimates personal devaluation is also the hidden but functioning criterion at the bottom of less crucial but nonetheless significant complaints. Highly specified markets gave rise to the professional magazines and the variations of *Playboy*. It was also the marketing factor which has made it difficult for family television programming, the public broadcasting network, and programs which appeal to senior citizens. Sign-carrying protesters against pornography are protesting nothing other than marketability, even though they do not know it and might refuse to acknowledge the fact. It is not the communist conspiracy which is behind the marketing of pornography—any businessperson will tell you that. And it is far from clear that it was the demonstrations of pacifists that ended the war in Vietnam; quite likely it was merely the cost-benefit analysis of staying in or getting out. A powerful American Secretary of State once threatened war in the Middle East—not in the name of Israel's autonomy, but for the sake of the American oil-based economy. Supposedly he would have had us continue buying huge oil-consuming automobiles and go to war rather than become self-sufficient in petroleum by producing autos which would consume at a rate equal to European or Japanese cars. His position was restated in a "born again" president's State of the Union address. The dollar remains behind the expropriation of our spirit.

A veil of illusion deceives us because we are lulled into believing that principles motivate us rather than profit. Yet, if we were honest with ourselves corporately and individually, we could acknowledge how we actually live according to a commodity-ethics. We consume what is marketable and we are marketable according to our powers of consumption. "You are what you eat." "More is better." "What does your car say about you?" We consume ideas, junk foods, news, the latest unneeded plastic gadget, or other persons. Anything has the potential for being sold, once a need can be artificially created and then identified with a marketable commodity.

Friendship, intimacy, love, pride, happiness, and joy are actually the *objects* we buy and consume, much more so than the tubes, liquor bottles, Cadillacs, and Buicks that promise them and bear their names. And since none of these deepest human hopes can be fulfilled in any product, the mere consumption of them is never enough; "more" of the product, or a "new improved" product, is the only relief offered to our human longings. Thus the seller drives us to greater purchasing with even more extravagantly concocted promises: more commodities as the solution to anxiety stimulated by media manipulation. Consumption, consequently, is not just an economic factor. It emerges as a "way of life." It is an addiction.

Is it any wonder, then, that one-sixth of the world continues to struggle mightily to consume up to half of the world's energy and a third of its food, or that a nation could have more radios than people, more television sets than homes or families, and more cars per family than children? When the Commodity Form of valuation approaches full dominance, consumption inevitably becomes more important than life itself. And the sacred phrases about quality of life collapse into meaning little more than quantity of consumption.

Our "life boat" ethicians are willing to abandon drowning nations or toss unproductive peoples over the edges of humanity's lifeboat supposedly because we are all facing the "difficult questions" of there not being enough to go around. Yet the hidden reality behind their perversions of language is that we are actually on a luxury liner sinking from the sheer weight of our automobiles, televisions, empty foods, fertilizers for golf courses and cemeteries, and parakeet diapers. We are terrified at the prospect of people having children, but we inexplicably entrust ourselves to machinery which consumes most of the non-renewable natural resources we supposedly fear depleting.

Paradoxical realities cloud and crowd our consciousness: we fear the mention of new life and whisper of population "explosions," yet even if the most horrible 1960 predictions of population expansion in the United States would have held true until the year 2000, we still could have fit every American into the front seats of our automobiles. We have become biased against our very personhood. A person, who challenges us to relate in mutuality and responsibility, is more threatening, makes more claims on our being, than some "thing" we can call our own. We will clean up after our pets, groom them, and lovingly wash them and feed them, we will manicure our lawns and meticulously clean the grime from our cars—but, we are repulsed at the thought of doing the same for our disabled old, who have given us our culture, our lives, and our substance.

The commodification of our desires, our values, and ultimately our selves, is, in its most blatant instance, underwritten by our television industry. Although we do have five radios per home in the United States, and although over 80 million of our autos are equipped with them, it is indeed television which influences most pervasively our commodity consciousness. Estimates of the average American watching-time run from 26 hours a week to the equivalent of 13 straight continuous years of our average life span. Since up to 27 percent of prime time can be given to advertisement, we could possibly spend, on an average, the equivalent of three solid years of our lives watching solely commercials. And this is their relentless message which assaults the self-worth and perceptions of millions: your hair is too long, your hair is too short, your skin is too light or too dark, your smells are noxious, you are too fat, too thin, too blemished, you must have a training bra in fifth grade or you will have no friends, your breasts are too large or frightfully small, you can stop traffic in a Maidenform bra, you will be frigid or impotent if you do not use Hai Karate or Musk. Our narcissistic buying is motivated by an anomalous self-loathing.

If we believe that this assault has no effect upon us, then we should be especially attentive to the way children watch television, the way they are channeled and manipulated in their values, tastes, and demands, and the way they can be convinced that they are miserable without the latest piece of junk for Christmas. Fifty billion dollars a year is not spent on advertising because it is ineffective. And in the face of such expenditures (and the profound, obvious trust in the power of advertising and behavior modification) the claims that the violent or banal content of television programming have no effect upon the behavior of children have a disconcerting hollowness, if not the ring of deceit.

Research by the University of Southern California has determined that elementary students experience a drop in all but verbal creative abilities when they are exposed to intensive television watching. In other studies, children have been found to be more aggressive in interpersonal relationships, more passive in self-initiating behavior, more hyperactive in nervous action, and more regressive in living and enjoying life as a result of television. From our earliest years, our ways of perceiving ourselves, our value, our self-acceptance, and our behavior are molded into commodity-like forms. The average pre-kindergartener spends 64 percent of his or her waking time watching television game shows (the content is often a combination of wild, heart-throbbing avarice in competition for money or commodities), soap operas (the principal characters of which are often identified by small children with their own parents), cartooned violence sponsored by empty junk foods, and frustrating commercials devoted to convincing them that they are despicable and desperate creatures who can achieve peace and happiness only in possessing and consuming products.

With such consumption propaganda and our consequent obsession for things, it is no surprise that if the rest of the world consumed and wasted at our rate all known world resources would be lost within one generation. It is no surprise that we see the population crisis as a question of survival: *they* must stop propagating, *they* are better off dead, else *we* cannot continue to survive as infinitely open consumers. The compulsion to consume has become for us as deep as the exigency to survive because the Commodity Form reveals our very being and purpose as calculable solely in terms of what we possess, measureable solely by what we have and take. We *are* only insofar as we possess. We are *what* we possess. We are, consequently, possessed by our possessions, produced by our products. Remade in the image and likeness of our own handiwork, we are revealed as commodities. Idolatry exacts its full price from us. We are robbed of our very humanity.

Our fifteen year old "Amys" whose lives are prematurely lost in one way or another have learned their commodity-gospel lessons well. And the American Fairy Tale of consumption, competition, and marketing one's personhood lives on—not only in our children's sense of loss, but also in the loss of our own selves.

CHAPTER FOUR

MISSING PERSONS

KNOWING AND BEING KNOWN AS A COMMODITY

Marketing and consuming infiltrate every aspect of our lives and behavior. They filter all experience we have of ourselves. They become the standard of our final worth. Marketing and consuming ultimately reveal us to ourselves as things; and if we find ourselves revealed as things it will follow that our diverse capacities for knowing are reduced to the truncated conditions of thing-like or commodity knowledge. I am not merely trying to point out here that knowledge itself has become a salable commodity, or that our universities have been compared to product-manufacturing industries. What I am speaking of is a more subtle collapsing of human knowing into models and patterns which are more appropriate to cognition of things or commodities.

A thing does not possess, nor is it known by self-reflection, internal consciousness, or any other method of interiority. Instrumental intelligence, technical knowledge, or quasi-mechanical cognition characterize our knowing of a thing. These qualities also characterize "knowing" *by* a thing, and it is on this level that some scientists have attributed "intelligence" to computers. Interiority or self-reflection is rarely being recognized as the distinctively radical foundation of human intellectual knowledge. The basic ways of knowing an object are external observation, external measurement, prediction, manipulation, and quantification —the most suitable cognitive tools for dealing with the producing, buying, and selling of commodities.

In the world of the Commodity Form, thing-like knowing has become the sole criterion for determining reliable knowledge about human persons and even one's knowledge of oneself. This is true of the behavioral sciences and their still increasing emphasis upon quantification in economics, social science, psychology, and the philosophy of the human sciences. It is true of the criteria we employ to evaluate the quality and promise of students. And it is also, and more significantly, true of the criteria we use to weigh the reliability of our personal experience.

The texture and nature of our immediate experiences (the condition of any scientific knowledge in the first place), our consciousness of freedom, our experiences of love, compassion, and hope, our longing for fidelity or equity, are all called into question because they cannot be verified by the methods of instrumental commodity-knowledge. The intense skepticism concerning our most intimately human thoughts and feelings is in considerable part caused by reducing human knowledge to technical intelligence. We take for granted that technical intelligence is some grand historic leap forward in humanity's ongoing rush to perfection. And we do not even suspect that such an imperialism of object-knowledge over our consciousness might be related to the rise of advanced industrial capitalism and the enthronement of the commodity as the center of our lives. We do not consider the possibility that the dominance of thing-knowledge goes hand in hand with an ideology that has substituted consumption and marketing for the development and realization of human persons.

Faith in a person as well as faith in an ideal, in a future possibility, or even in ourselves—the very forms of knowledge which yield newness or solicit commitment in life, work, and love—are banished from a constricted world of measurement, quantification, and external observation. These personal forms of knowledge are marked by an inescapable vulnerability and risk which cannot be scientifically apprehended or resolved. Risk and mystery, inherent to personal encounter, are precisely the aspects of living and knowing which must be minimized in thing-knowledge.

Consequently, if technical scientific knowledge or instrumental reason is the *ultimate* criterion of reliable knowledge, then human experience, and the forms of knowing, such as intuition, feeling, emotion, aesthetic judgment, sensuousness, wisdom, purposefulness and ethical judgment, can all be dogmatically passed off (as B. F. Skinner does in *Science and Human Behavior*) as "prescientific." Even more destructively, the most human dimensions of our knowing are subjected to a skeptical erosion of confidence. The personal experience of being loved or being believed in, the act of trusting or caring for another person, the knowledge of certain moral principles concerning human dignity and potentiality, all become inaccessible when only thing-type knowledge is acceptable. The "peak experiences" of our lives, experiences which Abraham Maslow pointed out as being founded upon a non-quantifiable, non-technically-controllable "being-cognition," are often described as scientifically immature or unreliable forms of knowing. Only the publicly verifiable and repeatable, only the measurable experience, is regarded as truly trustworthy. Thus, in thingified knowledge, what is most human in us becomes most alien to us, its possibility having been defined out of existence in a universe of discourse whose perimeters are established by the limits of thinghood.

The commodification of human knowledge has far-reaching implications, whether it be in the postured "value free" investigations of scientific experimentation or in a child's estimation of self-worth through quantity and competition measurement. The formative influence of capitalism and ever-expanding consumption upon our categories of thought and experience is not called into question; our humanity is. At the deepest reaches of our self-consciousness, thing-knowledge achieves its most stunning impact upon the ways we have become possessed by our commodities. Trusting most wholeheartedly in commodity-formed knowledge, we begin to understand and recreate ourselves in the image and likeness of the products of our hands. In our popular scientism, in our literature and art, we are most mystical about things. We are most mechanistic when we speak of persons.

VALUING AND WILLING
UNDER THE COMMODITY FORM

As we know, so we act. And human action, throughout a spectrum ranging from the geopolitical to the most intimate, is modeled after the things which possess us and the thing-knowledge in which we have immersed ourselves as the sole criterion of our self-understanding. In the behavioral area of ethics and morals the connection is most immediately evident. Skepticism and relativism in ethics are the necessary correlatives of personal skepticism in our self-understanding. Morality, once it is restricted by the categories of measurement, description, observation, and quantity, becomes reduced to a by-product of custom, utility, force, and the free market of preference. This is a consequence of the supremacy of the commodity-as-moral reality, but it is also bolstered by the more extensive cognitive dimensions of the Commodity Form mentioned above.

Moral relativism is the ethical embodiment of *laissez faire* economics: non-interference from the centralized agency of our personhood or from our common, objectively shared humanity with its natural potentialities seeking to be realized. Moral relativism, like *laissez faire* economics, is non-communitarian, it is non-sharing, it is isolationist, and it is rampantly individualistic. "You do your thing and I do mine," a phrase of self-styled cultural liberation, is in no way a challenge to capitalism or the traditions of the Commodity Form. It is merely the moral linguistic currency of the mythical free market, regulated only by the marketing principles of preference and number, Gallup polls, social pressure, encrusted custom, or the ruling ideas of the ruling class.

What we are not aware of and do not question is what *makes* "my thing" mine. Is it most intimately and humanly mine, or is it my idiosyncratic and blind introjection of competition, hedonism, and marketability? When hidden by the veil of illusion, ethics are helplessly subjected to the laws of selling, to the dialectics of supply and demand, to the play of respectability's market. Thus, in our discussions of wiping out prisoners on death row, of eliminating unwanted children, of manipulating South American economies, of soiling the environment, neglecting the old, and escalating the arms race, morality is easily relativized according to the canons of expediency. The most shrill immediate need, the popularly accepted dogma, the institutionally supported prejudices, the pragmatic and the profitable, are the norms of commodity ethics.

Taking a moral stance has become an increasingly rare phenomenon. Unsure of the most primal laws of human personhood, trusting in number and production, our ethical commitments weaken as our moral sense of the irreplaceable person capable of self-understanding and judgment slowly erodes. No power of number or social acceptance could have established the interior grounds of resistance to racism in the United States in the 1940s or to the anti-Semitism of the Third Reich. It was precisely the marketability, the social acceptability, the feasible technical rationality, and the money value of racism and anti-Semitism which legitimated their very being and made so difficult an individual's stand against them.

Commodity ethics, the ethics of quantity, relativism, and cultural acceptance, is the legitimation of what *is*. This is why we suffer such a dearth of people willing to take a moral stand on social or personal forms of evil. What *is*, is accepted or affirmed. What *might* or *should* be, is beyond comprehension, victim of a failure in imagination as well as nerve. Thus, university students today are often at a loss for words or rational discourse when you ask them: "Would it be moral to exterminate 10 million people if it would end all of our troubles, if 80 percent of our people approved of it, if the law approved, and if they were a lethal threat to our security?"

Commitment demands the engaging of human risk in the act of freedom; and it is the extinction of that act of freedom, ultimately, which results from the imperialism of the commodity.

The object, lacking interiority and subjectivity, is not free. But since men and women have patterned their knowledge after thing-knowledge, the inescapable conclusion is that they are not free within themselves, and *a fortiori* are incapable of free commitment to others. If self-understanding is not a legitimate form of knowledge, how can self-possession, much less self-donation in loving, be acceptable as a real possibility? In the absence of self-donation as the expression of human autonomy, commodity consciousness has displaced freedom with the myth of the free market. Just as our shrivelled powers of affection are invested in soap-operas and sweaters for poodles, so our lost freedom is mythologized into an "as if" reality called a "free" market. Our "freedom to choose" is between more products, between scenarios for success, between empty promises.

But we know that even this freedom is an illusion: it is merely a functional and culturally serviceable concept of freedom applied to a mercantile dynamic. It is a freedom controlled by oligopolies, a submissive servant of impersonal forces and conditioned-to-buy-automatons. It is a "freedom" appropriate only to a passive object.

HUMAN INTERACTION COMMODIFIED: VIOLENCE

We do not give invitations to or make requests of objects. Our behavior towards things is use, demand, force, manipulation, and, if required, destruction. Within the Commodity Form of life, since self-worth and self-evaluation are measured in terms of quantitative production, consumption, and competition, we are conditioned to relate to each other as things—or, more frequently, as obstructions. If quantity is the goal, conflict is the method. Our value and dignity are rooted, not in the capacity to perform free human acts of knowing and loving, but in the dynamics of domination. The interaction of commodity with commodity is not one of the reciprocal mutuality or the collaboration of subjects. It is rather one of price competition (is it true that "every man has his price?"), quantitative supremacy, and the power forces of commercial uniformity, control, repetition, and material exchange.

In this context it is interesting to note that "power" has become the byword of so many of the recent years' political-social movements. Student protests against the Vietnamese war were often more easily mobilized by the fear of the draft or the promise of a burnt ROTC building than by the call to a reflective and long-range commitment to conscientious objection or draft resistance. Many black organizations made it quite plain that while they were surely concerned with equity and justice, they were more interested in having a bigger share in the very structures and values of submission and dominance which had oppressed them. Many women's groups, while rightfully contesting the inequity of wages and false division of labor, focused relentlessly on control and power. Equality in violence, dominance, and machismo was often the underside of demands not for the revolution of a people's consciousness, but for the repetition and expansion of the patterns of injustice which had oppressed both men and women in the first place. The only change is a broader sharing of injustice.

This is nothing new. The "given order" has for a long time institutionalized power and domination in a geopolitical metaphysic of deterrence (the word means "out of fear"), balance of power, and first strike capacities, as the primary ultimate means of human interaction and problem solving. "Mutually assured destruction" is apparently the foundation of international dialogue.

Yet fear, force, and threat are not prerogatives reserved to advanced industrial nations or gigantic corporations. These values form the fabric of the "rising expectations" of Third World countries which must buy arms from the United States and the Soviet Union, of underdeveloped nations seeking to come of age through the rites of nuclear passage. These very values were the ballast of many "counter-culture" movements which lionized alienation, violence, hedonism, relativism, and manipulation— the reincarnate Commodity Form. Thing-like values underlie the shrill rhetoric of Christian writers and omnipresent commentators who sabotage every effort of the Christian churches to call capitalism, armament, capital punishment, and social inequity into question. And these values are the linchpins of some Third World theologians who call upon the poor of the world to take up the gun, to speak with their bullets, to reduce the dehumanized North American into an object standing in the way of a new imperialism.

Thus the chains of violence and domination are not shed. They are merely painted a different color. The commodity absolute can be painted in endlessly different hues. Within the almost cosmic categories of the Commodity Form, most reforms come to fruition as nothing other than variations of the dialectic of dominance.

The aspirations of women, the demand for the recognition of human dignity irrespective of race, belief, age, or technological sophistication, the appeal for the recognition of the human fetus's career of personhood, the resistance to armament and militarism, the reformation of our goals of infinite consumption, the appeal to the wealthy of the world on behalf of starving millions, are not the hodgepodge of vested interests and partialities that they might first appear to be. There is an underlying issue at the foundation of these demands: Do we perceive men and women as persons, or as commodities? Are people of irreplaceable dignity, or are they expendable before the altars of planned obsolescence, competition, ideology, and vested interest?

It is this foundational issue that is most difficult to apprehend, since we have in so many ways been subjected to the Commodity Forms of perception, value, and existence. Once a man or woman, be he or she oppressor or oppressed, whether dressed in silk or sprawled in a Calcutta slum, whether on a battlefield or in a delivery room, whether bourgeoisie or proletariat, whether criminal, president, or both, is perceived as a thing or in terms of the commodity, he or she is thereby rendered replaceable. The fetus is a "blob of protoplasm." The criminal is "scum and vermin." The brain-damaged are "vegetables." The poor are "like animals." The Russian is "the enemy." The wealthy or the police are "pigs." The "enemy" is an obstruction—quantifiable, repeatable, manipulable, expendable, the legitimate object of our hatred and violence. Only on this level of understanding can the questions of violence in the street or among nations, on death row or in hospitals, be adequately addressed as fragmented symptoms of a totality which itself so often escapes our attention and critique. Does a poor person kill a refusing grocer for the sake of property, for food and freedom, for security, for self-defense, for enlightened self-interest? Of course. So does a nation.

Critique and true change call for a massive personal resistance to the values of the Commodity Form which are encased in our institutional structures as well as in the liberation or revolutionary movements which would oppose them. The common denominator of most segments of our society (even segments opposed to each other) is the implicit belief in force, coercion, and violence—which are "as American as apple pie," as a black revolutionary once phrased it (not altogether inaccurately).

Many of the structures of government and education, the too frequently legitimizing churches, and the romantic rhetoric of their antagonists, are freighted with the language and methodology of fear, power, threat, aggrandizement, and self-defense. One can always find, moreover, the power-ethic of money and profit supporting legislated economic sanction for birth control, abortion for the mercantile purposes of greater affluence (not subsistence reasons), population scares, the threat of a Middle-East war, and a justification of national priorities by capitalist self-interest. Greater accumulation is the omnipresent, a priori "given." And its language is that of the absolutized commodity.

Once self-worth is defined in terms of appropriation, the cultural myth will relentlessly be one of materialism, property, consumption, buying-power, competition, and greater economic exploitation. It is this "gospel" with its valued "givens" which prevents us from *seeing*, much less responding to, the needs of the nation, the community, the neighbor, even the beseeching person next to us. We perceive objects to be used, enemies to be overcome. We no longer see persons. We see *things*. And things, like idols, are dead.

THE BODY AS COMMODITY: SEXUAL MECHANICS

If the worth of men and women is measured by the thingified values of the Commodity Form, if persons can be known only in terms of the mechanical, external, and instrumental, and if their interpersonal behavior is most adequately expressed in manipulation, force, and violence, then the world of personhood is replaced by the world of objectness. And if the human person is an object, the dominant form of body-consciousness in that world will be thing-consciousness. The body is a commodity. The body is a thing.

One would expect, consequently, commodified body-consciousness to be expressed in a variety of forms. There is the obvious marketing of sexuality in advertisements, the sale of sex in a variety of prostitutions, the high incidence of dominance-sex in the media's emphasis upon rape, sadomasochism, and bondage. At the same time we witness the continuing growth of what Rollo May has called the "new puritanism," an inversion in which love and sex are magically sundered so that falling into sex without falling into love is the commonest expectation.

There are three particular aspects of advanced industrial and capitalistic sexuality which are worthy of special mention. It is strikingly voyeuristic; it has a highly developed technological rendition of sexual relations; and it is marked by a severing of human sexuality from the totality of the human person, and *a fortiori* from personal commitment.

Observation and description are as characteristic of our acculturated sexuality as they are of our forms of knowledge. Sex, in fact, has become experimentalized and objectified by its reduction to measurement and observation. But this is only one aspect of the marriage of science and sex. Voyeurism, in a sense, is quite scientific, whether one is a voyeur of life or merely of sex. To be a voyeur is to be at a distance, to be outside of and yet somehow in control of the happenings (paying for or peeking in on the unsuspecting object). It demands no personal involvement, no commitment, no recognition of the personhood of the sexual object. It is "value-free."

Dick Gregory once maintained that the vision of sexuality in our culture could be capsulized by the picture of ten thousand men on Wall Street coming out of the offices at lunch hour to see a tight-sweatered woman maneuvering down the sidewalk with her forty-eight-inch bust. This is not an entirely cruel or far-fetched judgment. Whether it is in the flux of the free marketing of autoerotic men and women in *Penthouse* or *Playgirl*, in the queues of faultlessly tailored men patiently waiting to pay three dollars for a topless shoeshine, in the "jiggles" and "T and A" of our television shows, in the hottest-selling scandals of superstars' borrowed lives, or in the violent demeaning of women in our motion pictures, one confronts the voyeur culture. Behind such thingified voyeurism is the legitimating commodity.

Technical detachment and description (which are not unrelated to voyeurism itself) are hallmarks of the mechanization of sexuality, in which technique, performance, and how-to-do-it are controlling perimeters of investigating. In sex as in our lost self-understanding and ideologized scientific knowledge, final causes (purpose, value, and meaning, related to the question "Why?") have been subsumed under efficient causes emphasizing mechanics, description, valuelessness, and exclusive concentration on the answers to the question "how." Even the supposedly liberated books of sex education like *The Sex Book* and *Show Me!* are composed and edited like some over-fleshed "Popular Mechanics." Meaning questions, value questions, personal commitment questions, are utterly absent.

Our cultural romance is with the mechanical and the manageable. We experience an incredible poverty of language which could reveal or suggest the world of personal passion, sustained feeling, suffering love, ecstasy, promise-keeping, or the gift of one's self. It is true that Rollo May, Abraham Maslow, and even, recently, Masters and Johnson, have spoken of the inadequacy of sex without passion or the committed bond. But such observations are ineffectual without a more totalizing critique of culture. Cultural consciousness is saturated by mercantile media which for the most part reject any relationship between sexuality and human affection, and often identify sex with violence, domination, escape, consumption, exploitation, and thinghood.

Objectified sexuality is convincingly portrayed by the ideological propaganda of advertising. Specific relationships with husband, wife, children, and friends are supplanted by purchasable commodities. "I bought a wagon out of wedlock." "I bought it because it looked like it [a Gremlin] needed me." "This baby [auto] won't keep you up nights." "How to cradle your twelve-year-old [scotch]." "Think of her [an airline stewardess] as your mother." "A heart-to-heart talk with Climatrol Computer." The sexual relationship itself is reduced to cash value by image-industries of capitalism. Cigarettes and alcohol are substitute intimacies. Women are portrayed in magazines as relating erotically to their products. Men find potency in Brut, Burley, Musk, and Macho. There is a persistent suggestion of loathing for the natural body—especially the woman's—and for the natural, long-range heterosexual union of commitment.

Teen-age girls are educated by *Seventeen* and *Mademoiselle*, the preponderant content of which is advertisement and editorial copy advising the packaging of the face, body, and personality: "How to wrap your package" (Warner's Bra). "If your hair isn't beautiful the rest hardly matters." "Ecusson territory." "A new belt for your motor." "The twelve-dollar neck." "Having a female body doesn't make you feminine" (F.D.S.). This objectification of the body is the theoretical underpinning for the body as product, for a systemic attack upon family life and intimacy, and for the high incidence of violence in high-fashion magazines. Violence is the ultimate objectification. Rape is the thingifying of another person sexually, negating invitation and commitment.

Sadism is sexual satisfaction in thingifying the other. Masochism is sexual delight in being thingified. All three themes appear in advertising.

The connections between commodified sexuality, capitalism, infidelity, and violence is patent in Madison Avenueland.

1. We are objects. Our products are called "Me" and "Self." "I found myself in my McCall's catalogue." "It lets me be me." "The Easy-to-be-me Pantyhose." "What does my car say about me?"

2. Our bodies are the packages of our object-identities. Sexuality is the coming-together of things that "perform," "make it," "turn on," and "get it off." Our products are sexual substitutes for the intimacy we are taught to loathe or fear.

3. Since the body-person is a packaged object, sexuality can be portrayed as a matter of commerce, competition, planned obsolescence, selling oneself. More lethally, revealed to each other as sexual objects, we relate in objective patterns of domination and submission (Dior, Calvin Klein, Charles Jourdan).

4. In this process, the heterosexual covenant is discussed with ridicule in editorial content, while advertisements suggest: "If your husband doesn't like it, leave him." "My wife got the house, but I got the Sony." "We can marry you. We can separate you." And *Forbes*, the self-styled "capitalist tool," can run a cover story on the "big business of divorce." The disenfranchisement of human relationships, of the natural body, of intimacy, is good capitalism.

5. Finally, the disenfranchisement of activities and relationships unmediated by the market (solitude, intimacy, friendship, love of nature, family) intensifies the ache of languishing for the fulfillment promised in the new products: "You can Buy Happiness." "There is only one Joy." "Sharing, Caring." "Martin [paints] understands." "Serena [clothes] understands." "Have a Romance with Olivetti." "A Problem-free Relationship" with an AMC car.

In 1945 Aldous Huxley described advertising as the organized effort to magnify and intensify our craving in such a way as to stimulate the principal causes of our suffering and wrong-doing: it is the highest barrier between our personhood and our fulfillment. Eighteen years later, Jules Henry condemned advertising as the brutalization of human desires and the degrading of our humanness. And now, fourteen years after the first appearance of Henry's *Culture Against Man*, the worldview of advertising has become a national philosophy of life, supporting and supported by the Commodity Form.

Here, in its most evident and undeniable form of advertising and what it does to us, the commodity-fashioned universe dominates our understanding as well as our sexuality. Yet we fail to get in touch with its virulent hold on our consciousness: some conservative moralists are more upset at the sight of naked women in *Playboy* than they are at the economic system which objectifies women, which makes *Playboy* the successful advertising phenomenon it is, and which offers a view of life that is the full embodiment of capitalistic hedonism. On the other hand, persons concerned with women's liberation attack boldly the midgets of our society while they remain silent before the titans of Madison Avenue, who have become the greatest force for the objectification of women in our culture. But then how could *Ms.* magazine lead such an attack? It depends upon those very economic forces for its existence.

With human sexuality objectified, voyeurized, and technologized, there is little place for the full relationship of one human being to another. Sexuality as an expression of the self, as a *saying* of the self, as an embodiment of interiority, is lost because the self is lost in the dictatorship of commodity consciousness, in the world perceived through the filters of the Commodity Form. We have modeled our sexuality, our fertility, and our intimacy after the image of the automated products to which we have entrusted ourselves.

Our acceptance of our bodies is constantly frustrated by the onslaught of indictments from the world of infinite consumption. One's own body, like that of one's partner, is continually portrayed as hopelessly, disgustingly inadequate, marred by lumps and acne, scarred with stretch spots and age marks. Our breath and natural odor are revolting to everyone around us to such an extent that even our best friends will not tell us of the horror. Seduced into a fretful dissatisfaction with our bodies and with our loved ones, we seek that so-called "problem-free relationship." The planned obsolescence of intimacy and marriage covenants is patterned after the career of our automobiles. The average American marriage lasts scarcely longer than the average car. Our families aspire to have more automobiles than children. Sexuality is automated and mechanized in more ways than we dare suspect. As *Forbes* magazine, the "capitalist tool," said of divorce in its advertisements, "The *business* keeps growing" (emphasis mine).

Finally, the misnamed "counter-cultural" view of sexuality—as we have already seen in the area of domination and violence—has failed to call into question the depth-values of our culture's view of sexuality: it has duplicated the problem but in a different set of clothes. With the de-emphasizing of commitment in human sexual relationships, with the intensification of hedonism in a new form of repression (Marcuse accurately characterized the new sexuality as a desublimation which has actually repressed personhood, historical commitment, and critical consciousness), the "counter-cultural" sexual lifestyles are not really counter-cultural at all. They are the intensification of the depersonalized universe of the commodity.

In their denial of commitment, the new styles have legitimated the assault upon freedom and upon the capacity of the human person to make and keep promises. In their assault upon chastity, they have perpetuated the dualism of self and body, and have sold out the possibilities of sexual integrity and life-love to the merchants of rock, style, and escape. In the counter-culture's denial of marriage it has joined hands with the disco and jet set in weakening a powerful base which could provide children with the experiential data of trust, intimacy, covenant, and an integrity capable of suffering for love—the kinds of experience which might help form men and women strong and stable enough to resist the imperialism of the market.

A family which strives to embody the qualities of personhood can be the most primal and resilient support for resistance to dehumanization. Thus understood, the family is essentially counter-cultural and subversive. No wonder it is under such a relentless attack in our culture.

CHAPTER FIVE

IDOLATROUS APPEARANCES OF THE COMMODITY FORM

The Commodity Form is in many ways a world "view." It is a view *of* the world, a way of viewing all the parts of that world, including ourselves, our bodies, other persons, our goals and fulfillments, our possibilities. We could compare it to tinted glasses, which filter all seen objects in a prejudiced way. But the "filter" in our case is not merely visual. The Commodity Form filters *all* our experience, our attitudes and feelings, our emotions and drives, our perceptions, our behavior.

At the same time the Commodity Form has a specific content which it adds to our experience, and a specific result which it brings about through our experience. The content of the Commodity Form is marketing, producing, and consuming; and its result is a revelation of ourselves as replaceable objects whose goal and value is dependent upon how much we market, produce, and consume. With our worth and purpose dependent upon the commodity, we ourselves are reduced to the qualities of commodity: quantifiably measurable, non-unique, price-valued, replaceable objects.

The Commodity Form appears in every area of our lives, in all of our experiences and enterprises. It insinuates itself into the ways we understand our capacity to know—restricting our knowledge to thing-knowledge. Trust is produced and marketed, not discovered and adhered to. Quality is reduced to quantity. Knowledge is non-personal, noncommital, "value-free"—objective, in the sense that our subjectivity is mistrusted. Interiority and self-awareness are held in suspicion. External observation, measurement, numbers, repeatability, are held in awe. We consume our knowledge; we are no longer enhanced by it.

We have also seen how the affective dimension of our lives—attitudes, emotions, feelings, willing, choosing, committing, loving—are similarly filtered through the Commodity Form of experience. The paralysis of moral relativism inhibits personal commitment. We are taught to have the passivity of objects. Immediate gratification emerges as our only willed ideal. Scientific determinism explains our choices through the criteria of measurement, weight, observation, and blind satisfaction of need. Life commitments are deemed impossible by our media, by the arts, and by the "received wisdom of our day." Intimacy, trust, and desire for covenanted love, the capacity to endure for a dearly held belief, are all repressed. Such is the patterning of "thing-willing."

Our understanding of ourselves in terms of thing-knowledge and thing-affect is the link to our discussions of "thing-behavior." We behave like things because we believe ourselves capable only of thing-like activities. Consequently, in three crucial arenas of human behavior—the arenas of power, of possession, and of pleasure—the great moral struggles of our time are in actuality spiritual struggles of men and women in the grips of the Commodity Form.

We become expert not in the power of relationship, or in life-giving love, but in the spurious power of force, violence, and self-defense. Terrified at the thought of the obsolescence to which we as things are condemned, we perceive our lives as conflict, as competition with other person-things or nation-things. We feel we must make ourselves invulnerable before the threat of the other, who might overcome or replace us. Manipulative control, domination, and technique become our trust and allies. People are produced. People are marketed. People are consumed.

Possessions which might otherwise serve as *expressions* of our humanity, and enhance us as persons, are transformed into ultimates. Our being is in having. Our happiness is said to be in possessing more. Our drive to consume, bolstered by an economics of infinite growth, becomes addictive: it moves from manipulated need, to the promise of joy in things, to broken promises and frustrated expectation, to guilt and greater need for buying. Property is no longer instrumental to our lives; it is the final judge of our merit. So vast is its pre-eminence, it is worth killing for.

Finally, hedonism and escapism serve as opiates. Pleasure is no longer found in the integration of body and interiority, for there is no interiority in a thingified life. Immediate gratifications dominate consciousness. Our bodies, like ourselves, are objects, packages, tools, and instruments. Commodification splits sexuality from selfhood. And sexuality, no longer the embodied expression of our now repressed personhood, itself becomes a thing for exchange and price, a battleground for competition, a stage for aggression and self-infatuation. Voyeurism replaces intimacy. Technique replaces tenderness. Free commitment and life-covenants are stricken from the lexicons of love and sex.

Such, in summary, are the manifold ways in which the Commodity Form appears in and underwrites our cultural gospel, the idol of Capitalism.

Many parts of this total world view are not, in themselves, intrinsically damaging to our humanness. The best examples are perhaps scientific and technical intelligence, which, when placed at the service of human dignity, actually exalt and enhance the lives of men and women. It is when the ends-means relationship is inverted, when the scientific model of human knowing becomes imperial or ultimate or when it serves an end other than human dignity, that the transformation into idolatry takes place.

Moreover, when the whole spectrum of our experiences and expectations serves as a reinforcing system of ultimate thinghood, when commodity values are legitimated and fostered by a powerful economic dogma with its media, its advertising network, and its value-formative industries like television, radio, music, and arts, the commodification of the human person is relentless and omnipresent. We are actually educated and trained to behave and think like things and to relate to each other as things. Thing-knowledge and thing-behavior in turn support and legitimate violence and domination as the resolution to human problems of power and possession; and uncommitted, mechanized sexuality is offered as the resolution of the problem of human affectivity.

There are countless other dynamics whereby the Commodity Form meets and reinforces itself while oppressing human personhood. Thing-knowledge, as an ultimate, renders any act of *human faith* (whether in an ideal, another person, or a God) impossible. Faith disappears into the security of invulnerable facts and the capacity to control and manipulate the other. A thing need not, cannot, believe. At the same time, when appropriation, competition, and consumption are ultimates, *human hope* is rendered obsolete: if our hope lies only in the accumulation of what "is"—in greater quantity—true hope is extinguished. The very intelligibility of hope entails human risk and vulnerability—a reality qualitatively different from the observation or repetition of what is. Finally, *human love* is rendered impossible. The denial of commitment, the retention of the self, the escape from our capacity to give our selves away are nothing other than rejections of our capacity to affirm the other for his or her own sake. Love, by its very nature rife with risk, vulnerability, and freedom, can exist only in a world of Persons.

Underlying the gospel of the Commodity Form in all its appearances mentioned above is a concerted and systematic rejection of *human freedom*. By freedom I mean the human potentiality for self-commitment or self-defining gift, based upon our limited capacity for self-understanding and self-reflection. When we confine human knowledge to description, manipulation, and control, we automatically eliminate freedom as a possibility. When we channel human behavior into fear, domination, violence, and mechanized sexuality, we inhibit the mutuality of personal freedoms. When we allow scientism to reduce human action to external blind causes, we methodologically repress any discussion of freedom. When we embrace escape and hedonism as cultural ideals, we exclude free commitment. And when we deny the possibility of hoping, believing, or loving, we are actually prohibiting the exercise of freedom which is the condition of those very attitudes.

The Commodity Form, in effect, represses those qualities which are most intimately and most specifically human. Such is the meaning of Psalm 115 and the citation from Marx with which we began our discussions. Persons relate to things as if they were persons; they relate to persons—including themselves—as if they were things. Having patterned ourselves after the image of our commodities, we become disenfranchised of our very humanness. Reduced to commodities, we lose the intimacy of personal touch. We cannot truly see or listen as vibrant men and women. We do not speak, limited as we are to the repetition of computed input. We do not walk in freedom, since we are paralyzed by what is. Such is the result of idolatry. Those who make idols and put their trust in them become like them.

In summarizing the framework of the Commodity Form and its values, I want to focus once again on the crucial point. I am concerned with idolatry: the dispossession of our humanity in the name of our artifacts. I am speaking of ultimacy: thing-values which have no other limiting principle than themselves. Thus the following observations are important.

A. Productivity, marketability, consumption, technique, scientific method, are not evil themselves. They are beneficial to the well-being of humanity and as such are "graced" values. It is only when the relation of persons to production is reversed, when the instrumentalities become the measure of the persons, that the Commodity Form of life rules and ruins us.

B. The Commodity Form is primarily a frame of perceiving and valuing. It is not the only or total cause of human frustration so much as it is the foundation for a matrix of values which make human frustration quite likely. A case might be made, however, that the primary cause of human suffering, failure, and evil is the propensity of persons to turn away from the vulnerability of their very personhood and to entrust themselves instead to the false security of pretending to be self-enclosed things.

C. Capitalism is not the only cause of the Commodity Form, although it seems to be one of the most fertile environments for its flourishing. If capitalism is unchecked by any other universe of values but its own, however, it necessarily leads to the Commodity Form. It is, at the same time, extremely difficult to appeal to any other universe of moral values once the Commodity Form predominates in a capitalist society. Since the Commodity Form has reached such power and pervasiveness in our present situation, I have presented it as a dominating gospel or "belief system" in our culture. As a worldview and belief system, its dimensions have become socially authoritative, unquestioned, intimidating, and humanly depleting.

D. There are other instances of idolatry besides the Commodity Form. The collective state, the bureaucratic church, the institutionalization of the personality cult, are all equally powerful forms of human impoverishment under different conditions or in different social systems. The point of my exposition has been to show how the value-ultimates of capitalism in our culture reappear as a Commodity Form of consciousness. In effect, my aim has been to show why such disparate values as family, commitment, human life, pacifism, equity, justice, faith, hope, and love have become increasingly difficult to talk about, much less live, in a society that has systematized the worship of commodities.

Once having made these reservations, however, it is important to realize that the very nature of our economic system provides a faith challenge for those who wish to live the Christian life. In an economic world that is based upon continually expanding consumption, in a society that already has a superabundance of goods and services, in a society that makes consumption, marketing, and producing such absolute values, there are questions that must be raised. What kind of person is *most suitable* for such an economic system? What kind of person, what kind of behavior is *least desirable?*

When people, at least on a per capita basis, have most of their needs fulfilled, how are you going to get them to continually *want* and *buy* more? Is it possible that it would be more financially rewarding if people were conditioned to be dissatisfied cravers rather than appreciators of the goods of the earth? Does one buy more if one appreciates and relishes things, or if one is continually dissatisfied and distressed and craving? Is it profitable that dissatisfaction be induced into the life-consciousness of a people? Will the stimulation of anxiety and tension (closely associated with the experience of need) be economically desirable? Will persons buy and consume *more* if they have been taught to be unhappy, to be distressed, to be unsure about personal identity, sexuality, and relationships?

Another way of putting this problem of the commodity formation of self-consciousness is to suggest what kinds of behavior are not "good news for business." Let us suppose that you are a married person with children. If you are relatively happy with your life, if you enjoy spending time with your children, playing with them and talking with them; if you like nature, if you enjoy sitting in your yard or on your front steps, if your sexual life is relatively happy, if you have a peaceful sense of who you are and are stabilized in your relationships, if you like to pray in solitude, if you just like talking to people, visiting them, spending time in conversation with them, if you enjoy living simply, if you sense no need to compete with your friends or neighbors—*what good are you economically* in terms of our system? You haven't spent a nickel yet.

However, if you are unhappy and distressed, if you are living in anxiety and confusion, if you are unsure of yourself and your relationships, if you find no happiness in your family or sex life, if you can't bear being alone or living simply—you will crave much. You will want more. You will have the behaviors most suitable to a social system that is based upon continual economic growth.

The appearance of the Commodity Form, consequently, affects us at every level of our existence. Our fear of solitude, which is one with the fragmentation of individual identity, our valuing of ourselves solely in terms of external criteria, is beneficial to the commodified way of life. Our lack of intimacy, community, personally enduring relationships, our sense of competition and lack of solidarity nudge us into possessing and accumulating things in order to fill up the lack we experience by missing persons in our lives. Our sense of powerlessness in changing the social system and its disordered priorities only serves to confirm and support our economic way of life. Our inability to live simply, to enjoy life without a continual sense of craving and dissatisfaction is good news for economic growth. Our ignorance of the poor and the disenfranchised, our *fear* of encountering them in truth, intensifies our flight from our own vulnerability and the truth of our own creaturehood.

This is what is meant when we say that the Commodity Form of life touches us systematically. It cuts across every human activity. For there is an economics of intimacy and happiness: covenanted love is not very profitable. There is an economics of the vows: poverty, chastity, and obedience are not very helpful to economic growth. There is an economics to prayer and solitude: they are financially worthless. These are the very activities which are held up to derision in our media propaganda. We are taught to believe that what is most human and most personal in us is impossible. And with the continually increasing expenditure of time in relating to the media, we actually decrease our uniquely human and interpersonal activities. Thus the content and the form of the media reinforce the economics of the Commodity Form of life.

We might ask: can it be that when Pope John Paul II speaks in *Redeemed of Humankind* of being slaves to production, to economic systems, to the possessions produced by our own hands, he is not only warning those who may live in a totalitarian state? Can we in the United States be similarly held in thrall by a totalitarian state of mind?

Such has been the thesis of the first part of this book. We have looked at Karl Marx not so much as an answer to our own problems, but as a means for investigating the problem of economic idolatry and how it enslaves people in a total, systemic way. We have also tried to suggest how such a total system can be subjected to criticism only in terms of an equally total claim that might be made upon our lives. We are fulfilled in our creaturehood, not by making impersonal idols which will in turn depersonalize us, but by being faithful to the image in which we have been fashioned: a personal communitarian God who has empowered us to take part in the Godly-Life; the Personal Form of human existence revealed in Jesus Christ.

PART TWO
THE PERSONAL FORM

CHAPTER SIX

TOWARD A CHRISTIAN PHILO-SOPHICAL ANTHROPOLOGY

PERSONS

When I speak of the "Personal Form," I am referring to a mode of perceiving and valuing men and women as irreplaceable persons whose fundamental identities are fulfilled in covenantal relationships. A covenantal relationship is a mutual commitment of self-donation between free beings capable of self-conscious reflection and self-possession. Covenant as the free gift of self, the promising of oneself, is a characteristic unique to such free beings.

Various philosophers as well as religious thinkers have emphasized this "form" of human consciousness; but ultimately I will turn to the fullest revelation of the Personal Form in Jesus Christ, as I have encountered him in history, tradition, Scripture, the communal endeavor of believers, and personal experience. I turn to him in an act of faith—a free human act which is neither logically nor historically necessitated, and which, while founded upon the certitude of encountering another person, is accompanied by both insecurity and risk. I believe in him just as I might say I believe in any other person or in that person's love for me, but the content of my belief is that he is the fullness of revelation of what it means to be true God and true human person.

Jesus Christ must be approached as a totality—not as some combination of isolated personal experiences, not as embodied in dogma alone, not as the mere summation of moralistic texts, not merely as a historical reality living in a believing community, and not apart from his own history as a Jew and mine as Christian. All of these aspects have to be considered if I am to be able to encounter Jesus as a total personal reality.

It is also important to point out that the "Personal Form" is not the prerogative of the Catholic church, the Christian churches, or even revealed religion. The Personal Form is revealed and manifest, at least in some way, whenever and wherever human beings are faithful to their personhood. At the same time it is equally true that church people or Christians are not necessarily the fullest embodiment of Christ's revelation. Christians have at times been notoriously out of touch with their personhood, as well as with their Lord Christ. Moreover, any believer lodged in history and society is as subject to the pathologies of history and society as non-believers are. Quite simply, what I appeal to here is the revelation-as-a-totality that is found in the full dimensions of Jesus Christ. And that reality always includes in some way, when it is closest in integrity to its calling, the church.

At least part of my encounter with the revelation of the Personal Form in Jesus Christ is made in the context of my categories, my self-understanding, and my general worldview. Revelation is not made or received in a vacuum; rather it is mediated through history, both in the context of nation, church, and culture, and in the context of my own human career.

It will be helpful to clarify how I understand the nature of the "human person." For to speak of "culture," "society," and even "Christianity," is necessarily to imply in some way a previous understanding of personhood. This principle also applies to action and purpose, not to say alienation or human devaluation. All of our reflections depend to a great extent upon a philosophical anthropology, or general view of self-consciousness, human potentialities, human drives and needs, human realization. This is not to say that I must define human nature in some static, wholly invariant manner which can once and for all be definitely categorized; rather, it simply means I contend that humans have species-wide, commonly shared characteristics, exigencies, and inherent demands—all of which, if violated (whether in infidelity or in ignorance) lead to a falling away from true humanness or true human realization.

Cross-culturally, cross-temporally (under differing modalities of particular social structures and historical frames), humans find themselves in a condition of incompleteness, of being unfinished. This incompleteness is expressed in a striving for, a being driven to, the realization of our potentialities in a mutuality of knowing and loving. Conditioned and limited goals or goods serve not as final satisfactions for our striving so much as they constitute continual reminders of its apparent insatiability and inexhaustibility. The dynamics and structure of consciousness indicate that our very "being" is a calling out for fullness, a "being-toward," a grand historical longing, a stretching out beyond the mere givenness of our limits. What is, is surely often lovely, but never enough. Thus, men and women question. And in doing so, they posit the quandary that is one with their identity as persons: Why are they not sufficient to themselves?

What is more, we can be present to or aware of ourselves as contingent and incomplete—as painfully unfinished. We are aware of our history, of our environment, of our relatedness to both. Finally, we are aware of the prospect of death. Our self-consciousness introduces the possibility of achieving a partial distance from the conditions of our history and cultural milieu. We need not blindly accept what *is*. We can at the very least fashion an attitude of life-stance toward what is. The world is not only *given* for our immediate obsessive response; it is also, and most critically, presented to us as *problematic*. Thus, again, when our world becomes a problem for us, our physical and ontological incompleteness is expressed in a cognitive form of incompletion: the question. It is the emergence of wonder.

Persons not only question who they are in relation to one another, but they question what they must do, who they might be, what they could hope for. And thereby, moral, religious, and valuational realms enter the human's experimental world. Each person is an embodied life statement, a self-saying which is uttered out of each one's finitude. Such an election or self-definition is spoken to the future in an unfolding project-career of self-creativity. This life statement is made explicit in and through the structures of culture and history. Consequently, as beings consciously open to the future, as knowers cognizant of possibilities beyond necessity, as self-knowers aware of realities beyond the immediate, men and women are not only problems. We are, as Gabriel Marcel reminds us, mysteries.

Within the mystery of human reality, however, there is profound ambiguity and ambivalence. It lurks in the incompleteness which reveals both our fulfillments and our radical sense of absence. This ambiguity is discovered in the unfolding nature of a life-project which is in many ways "already" and still painfully "not yet." It is rooted in the question which is our being—a self-aware reaching outside of our centers because that self-centeredness is profoundly insufficient. In other words, we are aware of ourselves as precariously contingent and unfinished, with a frightening and irrevocable task of forming, individually and together, self-defining life commitments.

Unfortunately, upon the discovery of our precariousness and insecure contingency, we seek to ground ourselves, to finish and fill ourselves, by running away from the fragility of our personhood. We submit to the blandishments of threat and domination, the pathological inversion of our drive to know and understand. In languishing for security, we enter into patterns of ultimate competition and accumulation, the pathological inversion of our affective potential. If we consume, collect, or produce enough, we seem to think we could eliminate the risks of being human, of trust, of intimacy. But we find instead the emptiness of a closed, monadic world that turns upon itself in violence. Finally, we seek escape, refusing to commit ourselves, in the face of our own frightening unfinishedness. At times, slavery seems less terrible, and certainly more safe, than freedom.

All of these phenomena are fraudulent methods of self-validation. They are rejections of the conditions of our humanness, refusals of our scary finitude, avoidances of our freedom in the face of death. Thus we refuse to be who we are, by refusing the grandeur of freely knowing and loving, by avoiding life itself as much as death. In this way, each human person has possible self-negating dimensions. We can reject our destiny and personhood through violence which is self-hatred, through retention which is encapsulation, through self-maintenance at all costs, through hedonistic escape from committed love. Such is our fall. This is the underlying struggle of sin's drama: the rejection of our very humanity, the negation of our personal creaturehood. We refuse to accept ourselves as lovable creatures, who are not and need not be God. Ashamed at not being enough, at not being finished or self-sufficient, we seek a false completion in idolatry.

All of this is not to say that humans are basically evil or egocentric (in the restricted sense of that word), for what I have been describing is only one aspect of the ambivalence of being a finite person. There are, as matters of experience, natural "epiphanies" —moments which Abraham Maslow has called the "peak experiences" of transcendence, harmony, self-realization, and ecstatic love. Human possibility is momentarily revealed within the experiences of cognitive unfolding, when we find ourselves defenselessly open before the mystery of the "other." At times not subject to our control or strategy, we discover ourselves integrated and realized, in loving self-acceptance and self-donation, and in self-possessed commitment. This is the emergence of our true destiny as loved and loving creatures.

These "epiphanies," however, are tenuous, fleeting, and subject to disillusionment. The seduction of dominance and appropriation continually threatens to enthrall us. Our insatiable and inexhaustible desires seemingly never are fully realized. And our own resources—even those offered by a loved one—are often too frail, too fragile, and too far beyond our control. The human person is indeed, as Sartre has stated, an "infinite passion," a pressure toward the fullness of personhood—but a passion which, if it clings to and closes upon itself, is terrifyingly groundless and ultimately absurd.

CULTURES, HUMANS, AND FAITH

There are surely hundreds of ways to define or approach the meaning of culture—historical, psychological, and anthropological, but let us make simply an etymological rumination. Here, the Latin is suggestive.

"Culture." *Colo, colere, colui, cultum. Colere.* To cultivate, to tend and till. *Colere.* To dwell and inhabit as Tacitus and Livy used it. Cicero used the word to indicate a "fostering" or "study."

Finally, and our own cognate of the past participle suggests it, the world culture—*cultum*—has something to do with the realm of religion. Vergil and Cicero used the word in the context of worship and honor—as in cultic objects.

A culture is a cult. It is a revelation system. It is the entire range of corporate ritual, of symbolic forms, human expressions, and productive systems. It quietly converts, elicits commitments, transforms, provides heroics, suggests human fulfillments. The culture, then, is a gospel—a book of revelation—mediating beliefs, revealing us to ourselves.

A culture is a cultivation. Humans tend and till themselves through nature into culture. When culture has an independent reality of its own it reciprocates and tends and tills us. We become cultured. Thus, although culture is *made* by humans, it in a special manner *makes* us—to some extent in its own image.

A culture is our corporate symbolic dwelling place. We inhabit, our consciousnesses inhabit our culture. The culture is a human tabernacle, the incarnation of corporate spirit. It is the living expression of men and women. Culture is *of* psyche and psyche is formed *by* culture. Hence, culture is problematic for any "theory of the human person," for any approach to spirituality and faith.

The word "culture" indicates the entire expanse of the ways that a group expresses and embodies its reality. It is the product *of* men and women. Thus it is part of the human totality. It is *of* the human. The human is not *of it* in the ultimate sense of reductionism. The purpose of a culture is to reveal and confirm us in our humanity. Like any expression of conscious labor, it must be a servant of our humanness, if it is true to itself.

It is true that culture is most aptly spoken of in the realm of meaning, intelligibility, formalization—the structuring and ordering that is appropriate to the tilling and cultivating of nature and our nature. But our understanding of culture must extend beyond those categories.

A given economic system, a political system, a constellation of the relations of production, a network of power relationships can all be considered part of the cultural reality. They are in a true sense as much symbolic forms as are human artifacts and literary expressions. They are expressions of values, carriers of values, teachers of values.

A spiritual and psychic problem emerges when the culture, which is a *part* of the human, achieves an independence from living, producing humans, expresses only one part of the wholly human, and dominates the humans who produce it. People *serve* culture. Culture no longer serves them.

A religious and faith problem emerges when our very categories of ultimate meaning, significance, purpose, or fulfillment are dictated more by one form of cultural expression (i.e., an economic or mass media technology) than by human need, human purposes, or by the revelation of God.

It is important that any given culture be subjected to examination and criticized from the viewpoint of the human and of human potentialities and not from a fragmented perspective representing only *part* of our meaning. When men and women examine the context of their lives and labors, it is a fruitful undertaking to measure the authenticity, the humaneness, and the spirituality of a culture as expressive of and responsive to integrated human needs.

The identity, needs, and capacities of human nature call out for a culture that sustains, communicates, and enhances human relations.

Thus, the etymological beginning of this reflection might be concluded in this fashion: as *alienation,* culture is a frozen artifact against which the newness of human imagination is rigidly measured and against which the persistent human hopes for fulfillments, rights, and values are dashed. It is an estranged house—protecting not persons, but fragmentary forms of human life. In this sense, culture does not teach, it propagandizes. It is not a sacred expression of the human. It is an idolatry—in whose fabricated image humans are recreated and diminished.

As authentically human, culture is the tilling of history by humane self-expression. It is also the friendly symbolic dwelling place of the human spirit, whereby new generations are cultivated rather than repressed. It is, finally, sacred: a revelation of Spirit in time.

It is possible to focus on our human reality. This is the *fact* of what we are, our species-wide potentialities that can be identified in any culture and that differentiate us from the non-human. This is a received reality, what we are by reason of being human. It is created, but not by culture. It transcends culture and is not reducible to any particular culture. This is our personhood: our identity rooted in the unique ways we are capable of knowing and loving.

We may also speak of the *expression of* our human reality. This is the way we embody our humanness in different historical and spatial dimensions. This is active, the way we express and reproduce ourselves in a broad variety of forms. This is culture.

When we speak of faith, we can mean at least two things: first, faith is a human *act* in history. It is an exercise of human freedom, of commitment, of covenant. This act and the capacity to place such an act is not given to us by any culture, although it happens, is expressed only in culture. Second, we can mean faith to be a specific *content* of belief. This (like the act of faith) is a two-sided reality. Faith in this sense is the content of our beliefs about our identity as human persons, our purpose, our meaning, and our fulfillment. This is given to us, revealed to us. We do not make up this content, we receive it. And yet our reception is always historically and culturally embedded and conditioned, it is culturally expressed.

The Christian makes an *act* of faith covenanted to God in Jesus with respect to a certain *content* of faith that concerns the truth of our human condition and our purpose, with respect to what it means to be truly human and truly Godlike.

There are some cultural systems of human self-expression (including institutions, economic relations, social patterns, power relationships) that *foster* the act of faith (the covenanting of oneself in freedom) as well as the content of faith (love, service, equality, cultic practices, sexual integrity, peace, sharing, reconciliation, the recognition of creaturehood, the acknowledgement of sin, and the need for forgiveness).

On the other hand, it is possible that some cultural systems or parts of those systems *inhibit* and threaten the free placement of the act of faith (through propaganda, restriction of religious liberty, psycho-social manipulation) as well as the content of faith (by teaching competition, fear, violence, envy, avarice, lust, hedonism, injustice, egoism).

If we are to presume that, like Christ who is God incarnate in space and time, faith emerges in and is exercised through the ambient of culture, our problem of faith and culture becomes this:

how can we have a faith that is truly historical (incarnate), speaking to us and others in and through cultures and yet be a faith that is not reducible to cultural imperatives or cultural immanence? How can we concretely live a faith that is not domesticated or intimidated, a faith that is not confined to cultural relativism, a faith that can challenge cultural ideologies and idolatries, a faith that is not wholly acculturated?

We must always ask ourselves: How does culture liberate, engage, and actualize our faith? This is the question that most of us always presuppose.

But we must also ask ourselves: How does culture threaten, confine, compromise, and betray our faith? This is the question we most frequently forget.

HOSTILE CULTURES

Our history, our fragility, and the high stakes of our lives, are all further complicated by the fact that we produce. We express ourselves in action, in making, in thinking, both corporately and individually. Humans are embodied and embodying beings. In labor, play, and expression, we embody ourselves as individuals and group; in language, art, and societal patterns, we culturally exteriorize ourselves as community or species. Culture in its broadest sense is our fundamental symbol-expression. It is our fundamental corporate task; and it takes part in all of our existential reality—our incompleteness and contingency, our brokenness and ambiguity, our sin and grace, our pathologies and peak experiences.

In its fullness, culture can be the free undertaking of communities and peoples in world-building; and as such, cultural structures can be invitational to the individual, offering us a world of patterns and values which serve as a communal critique for our subjectivity and perspective. In this way, culture emerges from the freedom of the human person, and at the same time fosters human liberation.

Culture, on the other hand, exhibits a dynamic which can be an expression of dangerous human potentialities. As the exteriorization of human consciousness, cultural products can acquire the characteristics of an objective, pre-existent reality, and as a result are apprehended as an external force "over against" the demands of human freedom and open inquiry. It is true that objectified culture provides a patterned world of intersubjectivity; but it is equally true that its realness can inhibit emergent human values. To a closed cultural value system, the novelty of human freedom and questioning becomes a threat. Such a system interacts with situations and persons exclusively in terms of *its own* objective reality.

A culture that is sustained by and sustains the Commodity Form of consciousness, for example, will relate to personal reality as a hostile, deviant, or heretical force. Thus today, many Christian values—chastity, pacifism, family life—are seen as deviant, mysterious, or strangely primitive. Consequently, those who embrace such values often find themselves under such great pressure that they must either accept the reality of the dominant commodity values, or acquiesce in their own lives as laughably deviant.

When a cultural system reaches a point where the options offered to the individual demand either rejection or complete absorption, the system can no longer be authentically human, can no longer be invitational, can no longer serve the individual as a corporately embodied basis of critique. For it is now a closed system. It is ideological because its universe of discourse cannot be called into question. It is idolatrous because it enslaves persons to an objectified, non-covenantal reality. Cultural critical self-evaluation becomes impossible, since there can be no appeal to a set of criteria which are not reducible to the criteria of the culture itself. Culture is no longer the expression of humanity. Humans have become the mere expressions of culture.

Any culture, as a particularized human embodiment, is of necessity limited, concrete, and perspectival. This is even more evidently true of the various value systems within a given culture. Precisely because it is a cultural value system, its reality criteria and survival criteria are intrinsically limited by its own concreteness and perspective. Consequently, once its particular languages, educational and political systems, academies of art and music, and "worldviews" achieve status as realities "out there," they (through human adherents) accept, judge, or reject other perspectives in terms of their own perspective; and any "newness" tolerated is only in terms of self-proliferation, quantitative growth, subtraction, addition, and multiplication of what already *is*. Any novel form of communication, artistry, learning, or belief must be either "co-opted" by what is, be assessed as revolutionarily counter-cultural, tolerated as inconsequential deviance, or, if the threat is great enough, eliminated. Faded jeans, long hair, and flare pants are easily enough absorbed by Madison Avenue to its own profit. Hysterical militants can eventually be rounded up. Religious sects and enthusiasts, if they have not bought all of the American Dream, can be accepted on the fringe with a bemused smile.

But what do you do with the powerful human drive toward personal love, personal knowing, faith, hope, love, and commitment in fidelity? They have to be explained away, negatively enforced, or denied legitimacy in terms of the Commodity Form. The first half of our investigation has been an attempt to describe such a phenomenon.

A culture, when it is sustained by a monolithic worldview such as the Commodity Form, is particularly adept at reinforcing the pathologies of knowing and loving. It is the nature of idolatry and ideology to call persons away from the precariousness of their unfinished free condition. The Commodity Form's ideology is "already." It is closed, complete, finished. The only newness is repetition. The ideology of the commodity is not open to invitation, free commitments, or questioning. It relates to men and women in terms of demand, manipulation. It relates to other social systems in terms of pragmatics, utility, domination, and aggression.

An idolatrous ideology channels affectivity and choice into adaptation, assimilation, encapsulation, and servitude. It is a culturally systemic rejection of human freedom and contingency. But in the flight from human frailty into the arms of pseudo-security and false fulfillments, the repression of our ontological poverty explodes into domination, explodes into violence within society and violence against other societies. In our cultural gospel, as in all idolatry, relief from the anxieties of personhood is pursued; but it is further bondage which is found. We encase ourselves in a denial of our authentic humanness, of openness, of invitation, and of risky vulnerability.

Certainly, I have been discussing "culture" only in its most hardened form of ideology. But it must be noted that the only force which could *prevent* such a hardening would be a fidelity to culture-transcending values, values not reducible to any specific cultural system, values grounded in the very nature and structure of personhood. These culture-transcending values have been the objects of a most relentless and systematic attack in the world of the Commodity Form. The values rooted in personhood are apparently on the decline, subject to a new form of planned obsolescence. The second half of this book suggests how their last defense resides in the traditions and lived practice of Judaism and Christianity, as well as in any authentic faith which might lead a man or woman to embrace and embody the Personal Form of existence.

CHAPTER SEVEN

THE GOD OF THE JEWISH SCRIPTURES: IDOLATRY AND COVENANT

I cannot claim the Jewish Scriptures entirely as my own or for my own. A Jew might, for it is his or hers, both as a personally complete revelation and as the living expression of a people. Nonetheless, I can stand before what Christians call the "Old Testament," accepted as a prophetic figuring and actual part of the revelation we find in the person of Jesus Christ. The God I believe in is incarnate and historical, and I cannot approach God's revelation outside of Jesus' own historicity as a Jew or outside my own history lodged in and nurtured by the Jewish tradition.

Still, any approach I may make has to be limited, not only because I am not a Jew, but also because of the intrinsic limitations of my perspective. Although I trust it is not entirely idiosyncratic, my reading will necessarily be *my* reading. In facing and reflecting upon the revelation of the Jewish Bible, I dispense myself from scientific, historical, and textual research, from a full explanation of how the "Old" Testament is related to the "New." Consequently, I will approach it in a simple way—reflecting upon what unavoidably strikes me as the message of the story, the Law, and the prophets. While I admit it is incomplete and schematic, I find such an approach yields significance and challenge.

One of the most striking dimensions of the story includes the fact that men and women are made in the image and likeness of a freely-creating God and that no other image of God is permitted than the human image which is the product of God's own loving handiwork. Everything that is created is pronounced good, even the man and woman who turn away from their very being in an act of disobedience to their personhood and their Lord. They would be like gods, in the promised security of controlling their fate and their call. They would trade covenant for domination. And the consequence was a falling against each other in violence or falling apart in disunity and fragmentation. Nonetheless, the continual promise of a God beckoning men and women into free covenant persists. Great figures emerge, willing to respond to the *invitation* and command of our being to enter into a life of relatedness. But more significantly, an entire people is called.

The history of Israel is a history of liberation: of being freed from political and economic oppression in the grip of their conquerors; of being released from the impersonal gods of nature, land, gold, or wood; of being saved from a mindless "behaving like the nations" in their self-destruction, their injustice, their lack of compassion for the poor and dispossessed.

On a more profound level, Israel seems to be called out of the most sophisticated forms of personal slavery: enslavement to the law, to the land, and even to the nation. Their history of covenant with their Lord is a history of purifications. The land, of itself, does not and cannot save; and that truth seems only to be existentially felt when they are deprived of the land. Nor does the power of nation save. It is not the power of armies, but the electing love of their covenantal God that protects them. But their trust in armies seems only to be shattered with the shattering of the army itself. Bereft of land and army, the covenant is reborn and survives in the Law, the people, and cult. But Law and cult themselves, if cut off from the covenantal Lord, can become as idolatrous as a golden calf. And so, in final poverty, Israel must be purified of an idolatrous law that has blinded them to their own humanity. It is compassion, not sacrifice, which is asked of them by their God. It is the law of the heart, not of stones or parchment, which the prophets promise and elicit. The covenant with God, the law of the heart to which God invites humans, yields not only a fidelity to covenant, but also the mutual recognition of one another's dignity and freedom:

> What is good has been explained to you, man:
> this is what Yahweh asks of you:
> only this, to act justly,
> to love tenderly,
> and to walk humbly with your God [Mic. 6:8].

Mere holocausts and the easy blood of animals are worthless offerings which are more a displacement of humanity than an expression of it. This God wants not the debasement of persons, not obsequiousness, not slaves, but free men and women, who recognize their dignity in their freedom of covenant and express that dignity in their recognition of each other's worth. Thus Amos rails against the trampling upon the poor, the extortion and exploitation of the oppressed, and the loss of justice while vile sacrifices are offered as magical atonement. Jeremiah (Chapters 7, 22) calls for justice and equity as the expression of a new interior covenant. Habakkuk (Chapter 2) warns against the treachery of wealth, the insatiable bondage to greed, the plundering of peoples, and the exploitation of the poor while towns and empires are built over their spilt blood. And Isaiah calls for a covenant that must be expressed in fidelity to human dignity.

> Is not this the sort of fast that pleases me—
> It is the Lord Yahweh who speaks—
> to break unjust fetters and undo the thongs of the yoke,
> to let the oppressed go free and break every yoke,
> to share your bread with the hungry,
> and shelter the homeless poor,
> to clothe the man you see naked
> and not turn from your own kin?
> Then will your light shine like the dawn
> and your wound be quickly healed over.
> Your integrity will go before you,
> and the glory of Yahweh behind you.
> Cry, and Yahweh will answer;
> call, and He will say "I am here."

If you do away with the yoke, the clenched fist,
the wicked word, if you give your bread to the hungry
and relief to the oppressed,
your light will rise in the darkness
and your shadow become like noon.
Yahweh will always guide you,
giving you relief in desert places.
He will give strength to your bones
and you will be like a watered garden,
like a spring of water whose waters never run dry.

[Isa. 58:6–11]

Thus, while the free covenant with the living God is a call out of
bondage and idolatry, the people of God are at the same time and
by that very reason called into a new life of relatedness—not only
with God, but with their fellow human beings. This call to justice
is the very embodiment and expression of relatedness with the
living God. It is a relatedness, moreover, which presupposes
freedom for persons. The Lord of the universe will pursue humanity with the persistence of a lover, a spouse, a father and a
mother, but it will be a pursuit that insists upon a free response on
the part of the human. God will not exact of us a blind acquies-
cence or subjugation. God waits for the free self-gift. As Martin
Buber has put it in *I and Thou:* at the bottom of our identity, we
are called to life in relationship.

The *Thou* meets me through grace—it is not found by
seeking. But my speaking of the primary word to it is an act
of my being, is indeed *the* act of my being.

The *Thou* meets me. But I step into direct relation with it.
Hence the relation means being chosen and choosing, suffering and action in one; just as any action of the whole
being, which means the suspension of all partial actions and
consequently of all sensations of actions grounded only in
their particular limitation, is bound to resemble suffering.

The primary word *I-Thou* can be spoken only with the
whole being. Concentration and fusion into the whole being
can never take place through my agency, nor can it ever take

place without me. I become through my relation to the *Thou;* as I become *I,* I say *Thou.*

All real living is meeting.

Such is the call of men and women. Out of slavery and domination into the covenant of intimacy with a God who wants them only to be free in their self-gift. This God is Absolute Person, and invites forth the personhood of men and women fashioned in the divine image. God calls us to a dependence upon nothing other than the exigencies of our own humanity and its reaching out in trust, faith, and love for Yahweh.

The revelation of this God, consequently, is at the same time an exaltation of the human person, of human relationships, and of the capacity of men and women to freely enter covenants of intimacy, exercising their freedom in fidelity, hope, care. All other gods are unworthy of the human, for they demand not freedom and personhood, but submission, blindness, slavery, and the worship of unworthy objects. Thus God is a jealous God. There can be no division of our final allegiance. In God alone, in God's love, is our final identity, realization, and hope.

This is the Isaian love, which calls us by our first name, which has branded us on the palm of the hand, which cannot ever allow God to forget us, which would not have us fear. This is the Hosean love, in which Israel's God would lead us with strings of care, teaching us to walk, holding us close, finding it impossible even to consider being parted from us. It is the love expressed in the Psalmist which would set us free in the openness of life itself, which would never abandon us, which would hold us with a mother's love for her child.

Only when we understand the covenantal and loving dimensions of this God can we see the power behind the Ten Commandments—the dignity, the elevation of humanity, the prizing of every true human relationship it reveals. No image or artifact is worthy of our final allegiance and worship: only the covenantal Lord, in whose image we are fashioned, is worthy of and appropriate for our ultimate and free self-donation. The covenant must be reaffirmed and remembered and relived—as any other covenant which is to sustain life must be re-enacted and re-embodied.

Fidelity to the great human covenants—family, loved one, parents, neighbor—is called forth from men and women. Sexuality is pronounced blessed, the sacred sign of our love and longings, an expression of our life choices, commitments, and identity. Human life is held sacred—without conditions. Trust is established as the protector of corporate life and community; envy and jealousy are branded as humanly divisive and fragmenting. The great laws of God are not, then, some list of frustrations delivered against the human person. They are the expressions of personhood in its fullest exercise and aspiration. These are imperatives for the realization of humanity, not the denial of humanity. They are advocates of freedom, not inhibitors of it.

There is so much more, of course, to the Law and the prophets that I might suggest here. But any reading of the Jewish Scripture will, I propose, yield a deeper realization that the revelation of men and women is found in the covenantal relationship. It is persistently a document affirming the unconditional value of the human person. It is a declaration of independence from all idolatries which would enslave or demean humanity. And it is the record of a painstakingly evolving education of a people toward the freedom of a most profound faith, constituted by love of and for persons.

CHAPTER EIGHT

READING THE LIFE OF CHRIST

THE CHILD

What is it like to read some time-worn text with new eyes and with a new principle of investigation? If I really begin an earnest inquiry, seeking out what kind of God, what kind of human, is revealed as Truth, what will I come up with? Or what will be my findings if I take up the Scripture with a fresh understanding of the Commodity Form and its gospel upon my mind? What might be my result if I asked what I could find in terms of cultural values?

I believe the answer is inescapable. The Gospel is the most counter-cultural and the most significantly revolutionary document one could ever hope to find. It reveals the meaning and purpose of human life in terms which are close to being absolutely contradictory to the form of perceiving and valuing human persons in our culture.

The gospel presents an image of God which shatters most categories that both atheists and believers employ; and it offers a model of humanity which is wholeheartedly personalistic, liberating, and ultimately exalting of human life. But let us just begin, and allow the story and text to speak for itself. I will, only because of the limitations of space and the desire not to be tedious or repetitious, confine myself, for the most part, to the Gospel of Matthew, in order to get at least a general sense of how one rendition of Christ's life and message is presented.

If we keep in mind that we are looking at the way Christ reveals both the nature of God and the meaning of human persons, what are we to make of the fact that he is the son of poor people? A poor God? A poor humanity? There could have been so many other options. Why not enlist the elite who could really change society? Why not use the benefactions of power and prestige, choosing a Roman family, or a different time, or some place other than Israel, much less Nazareth, Galilee, Bethlehem, or a stable? Why should it be Mary on whose lips Luke places the Magnificat?—stirring words not of mere interior piety or submissive quietism, but of exultation in the God of Justice and of the poor:

> He has shown the power of his arm,
> He has routed the proud of heart.
> He has pulled princes from their thrones and
>   exalted the lowly.
> The hungry he has filled with good things,
> the rich sent away empty [Luke 1:50-52].

At reading this text, one is tempted to ask if Christians have ever taken seriously enough the ringing "social justice" words of their gentle Mother; but it is more important to ask what is revealed about the God we say we believe in, God's revelation and God's predilections.

Luke, in his more extended development of the infancy narrative, announces the coming of a Savior to a poor man and woman with the words, "Be not afraid" (1:31), words also delivered to poor shepherds (2:10). The sign of his coming is the poverty of manger and stable, a poverty which, like the call to fearlessness, is reiterated throughout Jesus' life. The child is revealed to the entire world and seemingly all classes, yet his allies seem to be concentrated in the wise men, the poor, and significantly, the blood of innocent, defenseless children. He has enemies from the start: the armies of a King Herod's pomp and power.

THE TEMPTATION OF HUMANITY

Matthew introduces Christ's public life with the proclamation of John, a man of ascetical simplicity who preaches repentance, a conversion, or turning around, a revolution of the mind and heart. After Jesus is baptized and pronounced beloved of the Father, we find him led by the Spirit into the desert in his first adult encounter with the power of darkness that threatens his destiny.

The three temptations are particularly instructive in that they present appropriation, magic, and domination as alternatives not only to Christ's mission from the Father, but as flights from his humanity, as escape from the risk of inviting men and women into free covenant.

> And the tempter came and said to him, "If you are the Son of God, tell these stones to turn into loaves." But he replied, "Scripture says: Man does not live on bread alone but on every word that comes from the mouth of God."
>
> The devil then took him to the holy city and made him stand on the parapet of the Temple. "If you are the Son of God," he said, "throw yourself down. . . ."
>
> Next, taking him to a very high mountain, the devil showed him all the kingdoms of the world and their splendor. "I will give you all these," he said, "if you fall at my feet and worship me."
>
> Then Jesus replied, "Be off, Satan! For scripture says: You must worship the Lord your God and serve him alone!"
>
> (Mt. 4:3–10).

Thus are established the themes of Jesus' life and message and redemptive work. It is not by the promise or sustenance of mere bread that his kingdom will be achieved. Nor is it through the magical machinations of escape or spectacle. And most of all, it will not be effected by turning away from the covenantal Lord and worshiping the Power of mighty kingdoms. No, rather it will be established by service to the God beyond humanity for the sake of humanity, a service that never turns from Christ's own human frailty and radical dependence upon the word of God. Thus, the three temptations reveal at least two significant things early in the Gospel of Matthew: there is the suggestion of a model for human action, a morality which is rooted in our covenantal relationship to God; and secondly, there is a revelation of our true personhood in the acceptance of our ontological poverty rather than in a trust of power, security, escape, magic, and their seductions.

THE ALTERNATIVE KINGDOM

After the calling of four not entirely impressive fishermen as his disciples and the releasing of men and women from disease, possession by demons, and paralysis, Jesus delivers the great Evangelical Discourse in Matthew, Chapters 5, 6, and 7. The themes can only be highlighted: graced and happy are those persons who are poor and gentle, those who mourn, who hunger and thirst for justice, who are merciful, singlemindedly pure in heart, those who make peace—even those who are persecuted in the cause of right. Nietzsche seems to have understood the Sermon on the Mount better than many Christians. Christ reveals that human fulfillment is found in the *opposite* of riches (whether spiritual or, as Luke more directly says, material), the *opposite* of mere good times and absence of suffering, the *opposite* of being powerful, unforgiving, the *opposite* of war-making, even the *opposite* of victory. Nietzsche found this doctrine scandalous, and attacked it as the demeaning of the will to power. Christians often find it equally scandalous, and ignore it in a life surrounded by power, wealth, and military might. "His words are mere metaphors," we reassure ourselves, "pious thoughts too gentle for this world and the business of our lives." But these reassurances are the words of a gospel other than Jesus Christ's. He would have his followers not be assimilated by "the earth," but be the salt of it, the light for it.

While Jesus presents his doctrine as the fulfillment and realization of the Law, he surpasses the Law in the application of his doctrine. Not only killing, but even unreconciled anger is condemned; not only adultery, but even the deceptive desires of the heart. Christ calls not for a "balance of power" or deterrence, but for a turning of the other cheek (we now make fun of that statement, as if it is some form of idiocy which shamefully embarrasses us as having been uttered by our own God); he wants not only equity, but giving to anyone who asks.

> You have learnt how it was said: "Eye for an eye and tooth for tooth." But I say this to you; offer the wicked man no resistance. On the contrary, if anyone hits you on the right

cheek, offer him the other as well; if a man takes you to law and would have your tunic, let him have your cloak as well. And if anyone orders you to go one mile, go two miles with him. Give to anyone who asks, and if anyone wants to borrow, do not turn away [Matt. 5:38–42].

I have heard Christians quote "an eye for an eye" as justification for capital punishment, just wars, and preemptive strikes, so distant they are from the actual message of the gospel which precisely denies such a position. I have seen Christians rail against abortion, the use of contraceptives, and premarital sex as "un-Christian" (three activities which I oppose on gospel and traditional grounds), even though nothing in Scripture can be found to condemn them as explicitly as the commands in the quotation above; but the words of Christ above, so direct and concrete, are wished and even sometimes laughed away by some of these same Christians as being "non-pragmatic"—the acculturated line of argumentation used against any moral position. Quite simply, we must love our enemies; and nowhere by the wildest flights of imagination can it be found that such love could be expressed in death rows, nuclear warheads, and defoliation of countries. Such is the blindness which the Commodity Form can induce in human reasoning and, yes, Christian conscience.

After stressing the interior attitudes of almsgiving and prayer, Christ teaches prayer through the "Our Father"—expressing our relationship to God in terms of great human intimacy. His prayer aspires to the kingdom of God and the embodiment of it on earth, not just in heaven; it expresses radical trust in the love of the Father, it calls for human forgiveness, and it expresses final trust that our God is not some tyrant or trickster but a guide, a parent, a protector.

"Do not store up earthly treasures" (Matt. 6:1). "You cannot be the servant of both God and of money" (6:24). Trust in providence, not in production. You are of inestimable beauty and worth which you cannot earn but which is yours by birthright. And again: "So do not worry" (6:25,34). But what or whom, we must ask ourselves as Christians here and now, do *we actually trust? Where indeed* is *our* hope and security? Success? Money? Armaments? Nation?

We hasten to remove the splinters in the eyes of the rest of the world, in other nations, in derelicts, drunkards, prostitutes, homosexuals, drop-outs; we will not take the plank out of our own. Jesus calls forth from us not the mere words of "Lord, Lord," but the solid foundation of action in love—admittedly a narrow gate, but one which can be entered when we trust his love for us. "Ask, and it will be given to you; search, and you will find" (Matt. 7:7). The question is whether the search has been given up.

Christ's kingdom is then acted out and preached. He asks people what they might most deeply desire, and responds to them. "Of course I want to cure you," he says to a leper (Matt. 8:3). He is startled, not by power and prestige, but by the stunning ability of persons to freely believe. It is the centurion's faith that amazes him—and brings about the healing of the man's servant (Matt. 8:5-13; cf. 9:22, 9:29, 20:33). He calls disciples to a life wherein they have no security other than in following him, himself "having nowhere to lay his head" (8:28-29). He calms storms, hoping to disarm the fright of people, expecting of them, again, only faith (8:26). He forgives men and women, dissolving their paralysis so that they may walk as free persons (9:1-8). He eats with tax collectors and sinners, proclaiming that he has come for those who have recognized and accepted their needfulness, not for those who think they have no need of being saved. And he tells the Pharisees: "Go and learn the meaning of the words: 'What I want is mercy, not sacrifice' " (9:13). He is a person moved with compassion for the crowd, those harassed and without a shepherd (9:37).

What might these passages mean to a person who has been taught by and convinced of the gospel of our culture?

FOLLOWING AND FINDING HIM

The middle discourses, narratives, and parables in the Gospel of Matthew reveal to us the nature of discipleship. The followers of Jesus must give freely and give to the least person—healing, cleansing, giving not gold but their very lives. And it will be their lives which will be asked of them by an uncomprehending world. They will even be hated on his account and because of his message. But he charges them to proclaim the truth boldly, fearless and straightforward, solely because of their confidence in his fidelity to them.

Thus, it is not some pacifying homeostasis or legitimation of the given order which his followers will bring to the world, but an option which strikes so deeply at the heart of men and women that they will have to choose between ultimates, they will have to be "either/or," and they will find themselves confronting each other in this fundamental choice. Christ's call is to an ultimacy in belief, to a wholeheartedness without qualification or conditions. It is as simple as clinging to one's small life and losing it in the suffocating isolation of idolatry, or losing that life, giving it away, and seeing it expand and bring new life (10:39).

These words are for us, now. Thus we today must confront ourselves. We must ask ourselves the question whether such words have any meaning in our present world. We must ponder them in such a way that we will be forced to either own and admit the gospel of Christ seriously or merely entertain it as a metaphorical reality.

But how do we know where Jesus is to be found, or how he might be apprehended? How do we see or recognize him? He himself answers to the disciples of the Baptist:

> Go back and tell John what you hear and see; the blind see again, and the lame walk; lepers are cleansed and the deaf hear; and the dead are raised to life and the good news is proclaimed to the poor, and happy is the man who does not lose faith in me [Matt. 11:4–6].

He asks us to believe in the possibility that our senses may be reclaimed, that we may see and hear again, that we may walk and come back to a human life, that the poverty of humankind may hear, just for once, good news about itself. Such is the way in which the Gospel of Luke has Christ announce his ministry to the world: "This text is being fulfilled today even as you listen":

> The spirit of the Lord has been given to me,
> for he has anointed me.
> He has sent me to bring good news to the poor,
> to proclaim liberty to captives

and to the blind new sight,
to set the downtrodden free,
to proclaim the Lord's year of favor.

[Luke 4:18-20; quoting Isa. 61:1-2]

Jesus proclaims liberating news in the midst of our very poverty—
not by denying our poverty, but by setting us free from the oppression and blindness which would have *us* deny it and enslave ourselves. Like his own generation we can reject him, just as we can
reject our humanity, our neighbors, our very selves.

The full acceptance of Christ, however, and the full acceptance
of our true humanity, is not the terror that it may first seem.
When we place our security in the appropriation of things that
may so easily be lost or taken away, freedom looms ahead as the
greatest threat. If we have identified our very being and purpose
with the idol we hold in front of our faces, the breaking of that
idol in the act of liberation will at first be experienced as harrowing abandonment to our contingency. But the letting go, the painful parting, is the letting go of oppressive fear, the unclenching of
the hand to embrace what we finally are. The burden of this truth,
and humility before it, is not heavy.

Come to me, all you who labor and are overburdened,
and I will give you rest.
Shoulder my yoke and learn from me,
for I am gentle and humble in heart,
and you will find rest for your souls.
Yes, my yoke is easy and my burden light [Matt. 11:28-30].

Who do Christians believe is speaking these words? Can we
ever comprehend that this is God's self-revelation to us? God is
being revealed to us not as some tyrant and judge over against
human beings, but as a humble God, wanting only our liberation,
our fullness of life. This is the God-Man describing himself as
gentle. The Law, the Sabbath, and even humanity itself, are gifts
for humanity and to humanity. The problem is in accepting
them—even accepting ourselves in the frailty of our knowing and
loving, the risk of our faith and hope. To yield to the goodness of
created humankind, even in its poverty, is what God asks of us. To
do so is to be obedient, in the highest sense of the word, to the

Father. And to do so is to become Christ's brother, his sister, and his mother (Matt. 12:50).

The parable discourses, after a brief statement of the Sower's story, are introduced by a quotation from the prophet Isaiah:

> You will listen and listen again, but not understand,
> see and see again, but not perceive.
> For the heart of this nation has grown coarse,
> their ears are dull of hearing,
> and they have shut their eyes,
> for fear they should see with their eyes,
> hear with their ears,
> understand with their heart,
> and be converted
> and healed by me [Isa. 13:15].

Men and women, with their senses dulled, their perceptions clouded, become hardened to the word of God precisely because of their loss of basic human capacities. Thus the word of freedom cannot take root in them. It is blown away with the first wind of challenge. It is choked off by "worries of this world and lure of riches" (Matt. 13:22). And no one can perceive the power and promise of the mustard seed, the yeast, the treasure.

It is the desire to empower men and women, to help them recover their senses and their very selves, that leads Jesus to heal and preach, to feed and challenge, to dismantle their fears with "Courage! It is I! Do not be afraid!" (Matt. 15:28). He calls them beyond the magical divination of mere human regulations (15:9) into true whole-heartedness, beyond the mere externalization and ritualization of morality: "For from the heart come evil intentions" (15:18). Jesus is more interested in who the individual person standing before him says he is, than in what people in general say or think he is. Peter's commitment and profession of faith elicits from Christ the entrusting of the keys of his kingdom (16:18–19) even though the weakness of Peter will be made immediately evident in his rejection of Christ's future passion. Like him, all followers of Christ will have the continual struggle of fully accepting their humanity, their poverty, and their authentic power.

If anyone wants to be a follower of mine, let him renounce
himself and take up his cross and follow me. For anyone
who wants to save his life will lose it; but anyone who loses
his life for my sake will find it. What then, will a man gain if
he wins the whole world and ruins his life? Or what has a
man to offer in exchange for his life? (16:24-5)

The nature of such renunciation will be articulated in Christ's
"Eschatological Discourse" and his own Passion, but he embodies it in his discourse on the church and the following narrative: those who are like a child will be greatest in his kingdom
(Matt. 18:1-4); those who are not single-minded enough to turn
from all idolatrous security, even their own talents and gifts, will
not enter (18:8-9); his people are called to be willing to forgive
unconditionally (18:21-22). And if such forgiveness is expected
of men and women, it will also be given them by God—expressed
not only by the unconditional love found in the story of the Prodi-
gal Son, not only in the loving acceptance of the humble publican
or the woman who has sinned, but also in the endless pursuit of
one lost sheep. "It is never the will of your Father in heaven that
one of these little ones should be lost" (18:14).

Christ calls his followers to a life of continuously desired fidelity and wholehearted commitment. Our very God is found in the
committed covenant of marriage (Matt. 19:6). God's presence is
in a person's continence offered for the sake of the kingdom
(19:10-12,29). But God is not present in any idolatry or in any
ultimate temporal securities or personal riches. God can be encountered only in the free covenant itself. To choose securities,
wealth, or riches which do not rest in dependence upon God's
fidelity to us, is a choice against freedom and love and personhood. This is why it is so difficult for us when we are "rich,"
not in touch with our poverty as men and women, to enter into his
kingdom. And this is why even the rich young man, somewhat
confident in his following of the Law, goes away yet sad—unable
to yield everything in his following of Jesus (Matt. 19:16-24). It is
not an easy thing to do. We would rather win salvation with our
holdings, earn it with our riches; but salvation, like love, cannot
be appropriated in this way. It is impossible for us of our own
power. But it is not impossible for God to beckon it forth from
us—as God's own free gift (19:26).

God's is a profligate love, indiscriminately given to any of us—not on the condition of our achievement, but on the condition of our free acceptance. Even the latest of the laborers will be accepted and graced; and in such a dispensation, even the last can be first (Matt. 20:16). To bring this love to men and women is Jesus' mission and purpose. It is his service. He came not to be ministered to, not to be placated, not to be won. He came quite simply to give and serve (20:27–28). This, indeed, may be utterly confounding—even embarrassing—to an acculturated way of life. Such is our need for its freeing truth.

HUMANITY'S SELF-JUDGMENT AND END

If people are held under the thrall of achievement, competition for supremacy, domination, and self-justification, such a message, such a gift, will be difficult to receive. The invitation will be difficult to hear. It is in this context that the great struggles of the last chapters in Matthew's Gospel can be fully understood. Like the Pharisee offering his prayers of self-praise, the most difficult person to speak the words of love and salvation to is one who "has it made" on his or her own. If I have won and accomplished, if I am a "self-made" person—what need have I of gifts? I have proved myself and justified my life. What need have I of anyone to say I am loved no matter what my lack of accomplishments? It is only when I stand, without pretense, in my naked humanity, in my utter incapacity to earn love and worth, that I can hear the lover bestowing the free gift of love. It is only then, unlike the Pharisee, that I can be compassionate, that I can give true love to others.

Yet this is impossible when religion becomes the business of expiation and the buying of salvation, or when the temple becomes a den of thieves (Matt. 21:13). The human fruitfulness of love and giving becomes barren (21:18–19). Lip service is paid, but not the allegiance of the heart. Even tax gatherers and prostitutes, so aware that they cannot and could not justify themselves, can believe the bestowal of love more trustingly than the evasive, the idolatrous, the secure, and the skeptical. Such slaves would rather pay homage to Caesar, to the logic of results, or to exterior propriety. But Christ would demand that the self be rendered to none of these.

The strongest indictments in Scripture are delivered by Christ against the Pharisees (a title not so important for indicating a historical school of the Jews as it is for an image of the kind of behavior Christ found recalcitrant to salvation). The center of our attention in reading his charges to the Pharisees should be: What dimension of our own lives is resistant to truth? What kind of person does Jesus so harshly judge? It is those closed off to loving or being loved, those so established in power, prestige, and security that they have neither need of love's grace, nor intimacy enough with their own human poverty to gaze upon their fellow men and women with compassion, those who think they can save themselves.

They tie up heavy burdens and lay them on people's shoulders, but will *they* lift a finger to move them (Matt. 23:14)? They demand places and titles of honors, seeking to be served rather than serve. They would have themselves exalted at the expense of others. They are blind guides. Hypocrites. Frauds.

> You who shut up the kingdom of heaven in men's faces, neither going in yourselves nor allowing others to go in who want to [Matt. 23:13].

> You who travel over sea and land to make a single proselyte, and when you have him you make him twice as fit for hell as you are [23:15].

They make gold, offerings, even the holy place of God more important than the offerer or the God offered to. Titles and tinsel are held to be more significant, than the "weightier matters of law—justice, mercy, good faith" (23:23). Straining out gnats and swallowing camels, they, as we continue to do, make mercy and justice less important than uniformity and ritual. Thus, the outside is clean and impressive, while the interior is "full of extortion and intemperance" (23:25). Whitened tombs, filled with dead bones and corruption within. Will the Pharisee in *us* resist being encountered by such words?

Christ's indictment is one final attempt at revelation in the name of all those whom he would gather to himself "as a hen gathers her chicks under her wings" (Matt. 23:38). "And you refused." It is our refusal which is our condemnation. Even in the case of hardened hearts, it is not that this loving God seeks to punish and be proved right. God's love remains—but in the midst of our refusal. God's forgiveness is continuously offered, but ignored. Thus condemnation cannot be escaped, because it is a condemnation which is gripped in the hardened heart itself. The all-powerful God, committed to covenant with human persons, cannot force us. God has been made willingly powerless and poor by allowing us to be free.

And so we bring our destructions upon ourselves. Closed to being loved and forgiven, we close ourselves to loving and forgiving. We bring the "end times" of tribulation and destructive self-loss upon ourselves and one another. Wars, betrayal, deception, lovelessness and lawlessness become normative. False prophets, false saviors run rampant. Judgment will come: a self-imposed judgment upon humanity in the light of Humanity's Truth (Matt. 24). The facing up to our own humanity, to our radical contingency and incompleteness, to the fact that we are not God, cannot be postponed to some far-off distant hour. For it is only in the present, the now, that we live, and seek to find ourselves revealed: either in God and the fullness of human personhood, or in idolatry. We must be awake, for we do not know the hour. We cannot put off choosing. The hour is now. This is a spiritual reality. This is a communal reality. This is a socio-political reality.

In Matthew 22, Christ gave the greatest commandment of the Law, the commandment learned from his own traditions as a believing Jew:

> You must love the Lord your God with all your heart, with all your soul, and with all your mind. This is the greatest and first commandment. The second resembles it: You must love your neighbor as yourself. On these two commandments hang the whole Law, and the Prophets also [22: 37–40].

It is a stunning text, a request for wholeheartedness. God's is an invitation not to bargaining the wager, not to paltry oblation, not to earning a tyrant's pleasure or benediction, but to a gift of your self in love. The foundation of such a gift—and the condition of its possibility in the first place—is a gift of God to you; and thus the primacy is placed on the reciprocal law of *returned* love. But the second commandment is "like unto the first": loving your brothers and sisters as you love yourself. A most simple, and yet, paradoxically, difficult commandment. You do not fulfill the law or yourself by *just* loving God—or at least protesting that you do. And it is not sufficient to love yourself alone—as if that were even possible. But in the full realization of truly loving yourself, you love your neighbors; and doing just that resembles loving God. Yet it is also suggested that you cannot love your neighbor unless you love yourself; you must trust that the gift of yourself is even worthy of being and loving, if you are to risk giving it away. There is no final exclusion between self, others, and God. To love one is to love all. They are interpenetrating aspects of the same total act of self-donation. Again, our life in God is personal, is mutual, is social.

These supreme commandments are most dramatically fulfilled and explained in Chapter 25, when Christ is speaking of the Last Judgment. Here we find Jesus' own evaluative basis for what it means to be saved or lost as a human being. It is noteworthy here that when Christ is speaking of death, judgment, heaven, and hell—the "four last things," which have been and often still are important focuses of sermons and retreats—he does not base his judgment upon the criteria which many Christians have settled for. His is a strikingly different approach to "hell-fire" and "damnation."

> The virtuous will say to him in reply, "Lord, when did we see you hungry and feed you; or thirsty and give you drink? When did we see you a stranger and make you welcome; naked and clothe you; sick or in prison and go to see you?" And the King will answer: "I tell you solemnly, insofar as you did this to one of the least of these brothers of mine, you did it to me."

Marx in his wildest dreams, humanists in their most articulate flights, secularists in their most vaunted claims, cannot approach the revolutionary, the humanistic reaches of this statement. Nowhere has humanity been more highly exalted. The *least* hu-

man person—the dregs, the poorest, the least attractive or productive, the least wanted, the most homely, unintelligent, or un-
appealing, the most neglected or forgotten human person, is identified with Jesus himself, identified with God himself. The
identification is stronger than even that of our most important
eucharistic texts. And recognizing the sacramental presence of
Christ in the poor demands as much the eyes of faith, if not more,
than seeing Christ's sacramental presence under the sign of bread.

Empirical observation, measurement, or description will not
penetrate the appearance of bread to see the person of Christ. Nor
will they yield the face of God in the eyes of the poor. What is
exacted of us in both cases is committed faith and hope in the
promise of God.

Thus, the last text before the Passion narrative is one that
clearly delineates the conditions of salvation, the expression of
faith, and the intimacy of God's presence in our lives. Note that it
is not tithing, not sacrifice, not church-going, not even the most
meticulous fidelity to sobriety, continence, or obedience, that
Christ insists upon: it is our response to the least of human persons, to the poor, the sick, the old and abandoned, the hungry and
thirsty, the naked, the imprisoned and unattended.

What strange gaps of history, conscience, and understanding,
therefore, have been at work in us to trick us into calling world
hunger a mere question of politics, not religion; into calling basic
human equality and food-drink equity a phantasm of bleeding-
heart liberals; into calling prison reform a plot of communists
and muddle-headed professors; into calling the aid of refugees
some mighty beneficence above and beyond duty or even human
respectability; into calling the distribution of clothing and other
of our earth's wealth unfashionably utopian.

It is the Christian, the church-going believer, who must face the
words of Christ and then try to continue in conscience ignoring
the poor, the dispossessed, the hungry, the imprisoned, and the
homeless. For if Christians turn away from the "least of these" in
the name of pragmatics, hardheaded realism, or, the worst blas-
phemy in the name of religion, they are turning away from none
other than the Christ they profess to believe in. They are turning
away from the greatest commandment. They are turning away
from God. They are ultimately turning away from themselves. It

is not so much that our compassionate God condemns us. We condemn ourselves—clinging now and eternally to the smallness of our logic and our fears, to a shrivelled hope and self-consciousness defined by the lords of culture; to feasibility, affluence, and the commodity.

Thus, the greatest tragedy for Christians happens when they sell, ignore, or explain away the heart of their belief itself, of their very God, to the dictates of practicality, helplessness, self-defense, consumption, and marketability. Yet it is not as if the living of this truth has ceased to be. Perhaps the greatest benefactions of the churches is that they have provided the soil for continual witness to the actual values of Christ. The institutions of hospitals, leper colonies, old-age care, even education (though often lost in the massive dimensions of corporateness), have to some extent been testimony to the values of Christ. And often the greatest saints, declared or otherwise, have lived—albeit often in opposition to established power—such a truth. Even today, Christ's witness and Christian testimony continue to move hearts, nudge wills, and compel minds into the direction of whole-heartedness, compassion, and service.

But the overwhelming fact is that the values of culture so often seem to take deeper hold, strike deeper root, on our everyday perception and self-expectation. The message of loving even the least human being has been lost in the din of commercialism, in the clamor of anti-communism and racism, in the fears of external aggression and the loss of our world predominance, in the panic of over-population, and in the cost-benefit analysis of how to deal with the old, the poor, the criminal, the unborn, the politically neutral.

THE CRUCIFIXION OF HUMANITY AND GOD

Such a fate, it seems to me, was not lost to the consciousness of Christ himself. In his own life he was victim of betrayal, conspiracy, denial, and failure—even by those who professed to love him and act in his name. At the foundation of this denial and betrayal is actually the turning away of men and women from themselves as well as from God.

Sin ultimately is the rejection of one's very personhood and purpose. It is only in this respect that Christ differed from other human persons and is fully one with God—so radically open and obedient to his humanity and to the covenantal unity with the Father that he is without sin. It is in his full acceptance of his human poverty and precariousness that he is the full revelation of God, because he is, in the utter emptiness of his abandonment and trust, utterly filled with God.

> The word of God is something alive and active; it cuts like any double-edged sword but more finely; it can slip through the place where the soul is divided from the spirit, or joints from the marrow; it can judge the secret emotions and thoughts. No created thing can hide from him; everything is uncovered and open to the eyes of one to whom we must give account of ourselves.
>
> Since in Jesus, the Son of God, we have the supreme high priest who has gone through to highest heaven, we must never let go of the faith that we have professed. For it is not as if we had a high priest who was incapable of feeling our weaknesses with us; but we have one who has been tempted in every way that we are, though he is without sin. Let us be confident, then, in approaching the throne of grace, that we shall have mercy from him and find grace when we are in need of help.
>
> Every high priest has been taken out of mankind and is appointed to act for men in their relations with God, to offer gifts and sacrifices for sins; and so he can sympathize with those who are ignorant or uncertain because he too lives in the limitations of weakness. . . . During his life on earth, he offered up prayer and entreaty, aloud and in silent tears, to the one who had the power to save him out of death, and he submitted so humbly that his prayer was heard. Although he was Son, he learnt to obey through suffering; but having been made perfect, he became for all who obey him the source of eternal salvation [Heb. 4:12–5:9].

The passion of Christ, the passion of his life and his death, is the passion of humanity—a standing face-to-face with our own poverty and fragility. Our frailty, the passing of friends, the erosions of time, the risks of commitment, the unfinished and insecure dimensions of faith, trust, and love, are so easily avoided by our clinging to the security and deadness of things, by the mechanics and magic of idolatry, and by the fantasy of escape. But such a flight from our poverty is a betrayal of the true power to which we are called. It is a denial of ourselves, a conspiracy against the source of our loveliness and our dignity. It is a flight from freedom into the slavery of secure sinfulness, of unredemptive death.

Jesus feels this temptation with his whole being. But rather than run from his humanity, with its pain and its promise, he abandons himself in faith to the promised covenant of the Father. His agony, his sorrow, his suffering, bring him to the brink of abandonment, to the darkness of radical insecurity and dependence upon God alone; to the precariousness of believing in himself, in humanity, and in God, of hoping without the certitude of logical necessity, of loving without the assurance of payment. But he yields at the depths of his humanity's darkness, in the face of Dachau and My Lai, of millions starved, of love and life refused, of hatred between brothers and sisters. God's revelation in Jesus is not a blessing from afar. It is a witness to the fact that our very God loved the prize of creation enough to be one with it, to embrace our tears and sighs, to feel our hungers and pains of unfinishedness, to drink the cup of our longings and unfulfilled desire.

Thus the Crucifixion. Not so much at the hands of the people's refusals or Pilate's crudity and indifference; not so much before the powers of Caesar and Mars; but at the hands of humanity itself—in the rejection of men and women who deny their very personhood; who, convinced of their worthlessness and submissive to idols, cannot conceive the possibility of their actually being freely loved in and through their poverty.

In every cultural or historical frame, Christians must face up to the crucified God. We must ask ourselves anew: What kind of God does this reveal? Can this God who is most frequently represented as a defenseless poor baby in a manger and as a defenseless man on a cross be a tyrant? Can God be possibly understood in terms of retribution, of punishment, of fear, force, threat? Can the Gospels which have God constantly telling us not to fear be a message of terror? Or have we transformed God into such travesties by the machinations of our own idols, when we bear faith to our children and the rest of the world? Can this be the God of fright and tricksterism that we have so often entertained? Or has it been the gospel of the world, of slavery, of the Thing, and of Death which has contaminated our very understanding of the Lord? If we do not face and answer these questions, individually and corporately, we stand in danger of denying the crucifixion.

We also deny the crucified God if we ignore the invitation of Love's cross to us. Quite straightforwardly, can it really be construed that Christ on the cross would institute Inquisitions, Crusades, forced conversions, racism, the blessing of tanks, and "killing a commie for Christ"? Are we called to follow him, or the received wisdom of our culture? Is it he, or is it our "civil religion" that reveals what we might be as humans, indeed as Christians? Or is he a harmless image that conspires with the powers of darkness, convincing us of our lack of worth, our loss of compassion, and our impotence as persons? "Who do you say that I am," he addresses to each of us. This is a gentle God, a God who would wipe away every human tear, who would rather suffer the terrors of created freedom than leave us bereft of our highest destiny.

A final way that we deny this crucified God is by insisting that it is we who save ourselves. Christianity is a belief about what God does in and for humanity, not about what Christians do for God.

> We were still helpless when at his appointed moment Christ died for sinful men. It is not easy to die even for a good man—though of course for someone really worthy, a man might be prepared to die—but what proves that God loves us is that Christ died for us while we were still sinners [Rom. 5:6-9].

> The spirit too comes to help us in our weakness. For when we cannot choose words in order to pray properly, the spirit himself expresses our plea in a way that could never be put into words, and God who knows everything in our hearts knows perfectly well what he means [Rom. 8:26-27].

> We are only the earthenware jars that hold this treasure to make it clear that such an overwhelming power comes from God and not from us [2 Cor. 4:7-8].

He has said: "My grace is enough for you; my power is at its best in weakness,". . . For it is when I am weak that I am strong [2 Cor. 12:9–10].

I have been crucified with Christ, and I live now not with my own life but with the life of Christ who lives in me [Gal. 2:19].

As for me, the only thing I can boast about is the cross of our Lord Jesus Christ, through whom the world is crucified to me, and I to the world [Gal. 6:14].

It is by grace that you have been saved, through faith; not by anything of your own, but by a gift from God; not by anything that you have done, so that nobody can claim the credit. We are God's work of art, created in Christ Jesus to live the good life as from the beginning he had meant us to live it [Eph. 2:8–10].

Here is a saying that you can rely on and nobody should doubt; that Christ Jesus came into the world to save sinners [1 Tim. 1:15].

. . . Relying on the power of God who has saved us and called us to be holy—not because of anything we ourselves have done but for his own purpose and by his own grace [2 Tim. 1:9–10].

This is the love I mean: not our love for God, but God's love for us when he sent his son [1 John 4:10].

And so, again and again, it is no shame to be a frail and contingent human being. In fact, it is priceless to be so. It is, necessarily, to be loved into existence.

Denying our sinfulness as church and Christians, insisting upon our success, our power and pomp, our greatness, as the proof of our being saved, we reject the cross as well as God's love made manifest in Jesus Christ who died for and with us. Earning salvation, winning salvation, proving that we are good, competing for salvation, marketing salvation, selling salvation, guaranteeing salvation, are not only common expressions of the commodified gospel. They are rejections of the gospel of Jesus. If I honestly ask: "Where is my security, whom or what do I trust and believe in?" And I reply, "Jesus Christ, in whom the inseparable love of God is revealed"—I must then fully face the implications of believing in him and his gospel.

The agony and the death of Christ is the agony and the death of God, if we are to believe that Jesus is true God. It is as if God, beyond all human imagination, when deciding to create men and women capable of rejecting themselves and life itself, when deciding to give them the capacity to love, also decided to die. God would be a suffering God. In God's desire that we freely relate to creation and love, God was delivered into our hands. Thus, Christ's abandonment is the abandonment of God on behalf of the beloved. Not only would God love us; God would choose to trust and have faith in us—surely not in terms of God's very being, yet nonetheless surely with respect to us as the created expression of infinite love. God entrusts life and truth to us by making us free. God suffers the dying within our love which will not subjugate the beloved, but which will enable us to reach the ecstasy of highest joy: free reciprocation. The agony and death of God is not confined to Gethsemane and Golgotha; it is the measure of creation itself.

Christ undergoes the suffering and death of humanity—not so much or merely by identifying with the millions untimely taken, or the numberless starving and abandoned, but most crucially by fully embracing and being faithful to his human freedom. It is almost as if our God may have expected something too great of us in desiring that we be free, something too difficult and high. We cannot face the dying to ourselves that love or trust or faith would elicit. Better to pursue the securities of idols. Better to seek the unfeeling deadness of things than the mysterious dying to our smallness in a free gift of ourselves. Better to possess the cold but sure completion of machinery than to say "Yes" to the promise of a person.

And yet in Christ, both God and humanity yield to love. God suffers the risk of infidelity and love's rejection. Jesus suffers the insecurity of Truth itself; the acceptance of his humanity and his fidelity—even in darkness and incompletion—to the covenantal longing of his heart. And it is to the Fashioner of that covenant, to the One who beckons him in his deepest desires, that Christ yields and commends his spirit. In acknowledging his weakness, he finally reveals his greatest strength—the life of God living in his precarious faith, hope, and love.

Our yielding, our commending, our entrusting of ourselves to the living covenantal God, is the rebirth of our truest selves out of sin and death. Trusting in our God made manifest in one of us, we can finally hear the words of the Reborn when he says "Fear Not," when he gives us the power to forgive, when he unveils our true history and promise on our way to Emmaus, when he makes the greatest of believers out of Thomases, the greatest of lovers out of Magdalens, the greatest of leaders out of Simons. We "re-find" ourselves, not as mini-gods scrambling for the thrones of power and dominance, but as God-like brothers and sisters in a community of unfinished free beings called to the mystery of fullness. We discover who we truly are not by overcoming others, but by serving them.

CHAPTER NINE

CHRIST AND THE IDOLS OF CAPITALISM

THE REVELATION OF THE PERSONAL FORM IN JESUS

We have reflected upon one account of Jesus' life and revelation. Such an inspection was necessarily selective and partial, concentrating for the most part on the Gospel of Matthew and a few texts of Saint Paul. But we could have just as easily concentrated on the writings of the School of John, with its emphasis upon the Christian's stance in opposition to the darkness and unfreedom of the world. The ways of violence, deception, and slavery belong to a kingdom intractably alien to a life of suffering love and self-donation. The Gospels of Luke and Mark, as well as the early letters of Paul, also yield an integral portrayal of Christ and the Christian life standing in striking opposition to what we have called the Commodity Form.

I examined Matthew not so much as a mustering of proof texts as an attempt to be present to the broad and recurring lines of revelation. I tried to avoid both excessive literalism and the metaphorizing-away of the unavoidable challenge. In this way I hoped to show how an ordinary person asking the questions "How is God revealed?" and "How is humanity revealed?" and "How am I revealed?" will at every turn find the God who elevates and exalts human personhood.

It will now be worthwhile to review the revelation of Jesus at a higher altitude, reflecting more theoretically upon a general understanding of Christian anthropology, and then showing how such a view of human life and purpose contrasts to the view of the human person found in our own cultural anthropology.

As I have suggested earlier, in a philosophical view of our human nature the most that we seem able to do of ourselves—if we do not embrace domination, appropriation, or escape—is hold out our hands and our lives to the unconditional answer of our being's question. To be a human person is to call out for a response, a revelation of our fullest mystery and purpose as capable of knowing and being known, of loving and being loved. In the scripture of the Jewish Bible the Mystery of human fullness reveals itself as the covenantal Lord of the universe in whose image the human person is formed. Each of us is called into free covenant, to interior fidelity, and to a risk-laden life of trust in that Lord and in ourselves as our Lord's handiwork.

In the Christian faith, Jesus Christ is the full and definitive revelation of God to humanity, for he is the point where God and humanity coalesce. Revelation in Christ, consequently, is not merely the unfolding and making-known of what it means to be God; it is at the same time the full revelation of what it means to be a human being. Jesus Christ reveals not only the divinity to human persons; he reveals humanity to itself. He himself embodies the delicate interpenetration of human contingency and full Godlikeness. And in revealing both, he redeems the broken passion of created freedom.

When the Godhead is revealed historically in Jesus, we are witnessing a divine insistence upon the free response of the human person. It is a benediction upon humanity and personal freedom. God, in becoming one with humankind, does not manipulate, force, or dominate us by power or munificence. Quite to the contrary, in becoming fully human, God invites persons into a freely entered covenantal relationship through Jesus and their own humanness. It is in this act of invitation, this act which calls forth a freely given trust and fidelity from persons, that God makes the fullest revelation of divinity and of human dignity.

Consequently, Jesus Christ, the enlightenment of humanity, is God's self-giving response to the calling-out of the created universe, now made aware of itself in human persons. God does not stop and complete human personhood in such a way that the participatory freedom of men and women in their own destiny may be extinguished. Rather, God's revelation in Jesus is a beckoning to me to accept my contingency and to transform the question of my being into freely uttered exclamation: I freely believe! I freely trust! I freely give! These are exclamations whereby men and women realize themselves in their relationship to each other and in relation to God. For just as the revelation of God and humanity is realized in the one Jesus Christ, men and women are realized in the one dynamic of believing, trusting, and loving one another, themselves and God. Herein lies our utter uniqueness as individuals and our irreplaceability as free covenanting beings.

To believe or trust in one's self, to believe in another person, and to believe in the personal God, are analogous activities—just as the two great commandments of love are alike. Each is difficult. Each makes us face how precarious our existence is. Each has its nights of darkness, misunderstanding, and sense of absence. Each involves an unfolding and risking in the donation of persons. Each demands a vulnerability, even a dying to ourselves, in the admission that we are not our own ultimate center, validation, or purpose. Each act brings us out of our smallness and limits, our historical and spacial confinement, into the fourth-dimensional world of personhood. For what we have revealed in Christ is that faith, hope, and love are the very life of our God, communicated to and living in contingent human reality. Faith, hope, and love are the divine calling-forth of freedom from men and women. They are the patient, persistent eliciting from human persons of the irreplaceable basis of their dignity: their capacity for free covenant. They are the exclamations of consent to their human poverty and authentic strength.

The model for these existential exclamations is Jesus Christ, who reveals the fullness of the human person not in domination or escape, but in a yielding to one's own humanity and a breaking out of encapsulation into intimacy with the other. *Human knowing* is revealed not as manipulation, control, and mere external observation, but as the medium of full experiential participation in the mystery of one's humanness and an openness to the other. And the affective drive to do something—*human willing*—is revealed not as appropriation and competition, but as the inherent human exigency to give one's self away in love, in service, and in the joys of covenant.

Jesus did not flee from the tragic dimensions of human existence. He lived in the limitations of our weakness, as Paul says, offering up "prayer and entreaty, aloud and in silent tears," being tempted in every way that we are. Thus he did not flee the transcending passions of our life and longing; nor did he flee from the face of death, so harrowing to our frailty and desired security. Rather, he embraced both, in embracing his humanity, and he entrusted both his life and his death to a loving, absolute God beyond all human fragility.

The Incarnation, as well as the entire life of Christ, is a testimony received in faith that we are redeemed by a God-made-vulnerable in loving creation, and that we are fulfilled only in our irreplaceably unique self-donation. "Man only *is*," Karl Rahner has said, "when he gives himself away." It is the very poverty of our humanity, our precarious contingency and unfinishedness, our openness, our frail capacity for the risks of living and loving, that is our strength and beauty. It is precisely this poverty, so terrifying at the same time and so lovely, which Christ so wholeheartedly yields to.

The revelation of God in Jesus is the developmental unmasking not of a terrible God, but of a God who would "wipe away every human tear," of a God who is radically personal and communal in knowledge, love, and free creation. God would have us "fear not." God is within and beyond us, calling us to ourselves, but only on the condition of freely entered covenantal life. God is, consequently, Absolute Being—or better, Absolute Personhood —in whom we partake by the exercise of *our* personhood, to whom we are beckoned by the exigencies of our being human.

Such are the foundations of the Personal Form, through which men and women are revealed as irreplaceably free persons. Seen from this more general altitude, and complemented by our reflection upon the scriptural revelation in Matthew, the Personal Form can now be placed in greater contrast with the Commodity Form and the choice of a god and human revelation found therein.

THE CHOICE OF GODS AND GOSPELS

What is the nature of the fundamental choice that people make in our country? The choice, under different forms, is ever present to us—and it is made willy-nilly. There must be a bottom line to the lives of each of us. We are all driven to ask: "Where finally is the truth?" Humans will seek out and demand a god or gospel no matter what. The question is: What god or gospel is worthy of humans?

Earlier we have seen how in our own culture the Commodity Form of consciousness makes claims upon our final allegiance, how it penetrates our self-perception, our values, our hopes, and our purpose. We can now see more clearly how the characteristics of the Commodity Form stand in relation to human reality and to the revelation of the Personal Form in Jesus Christ. Experiencing ourselves as incomplete and open freedoms, we often seek completion in thinghood and the commodity. They are idols to which we offer our freedom and personhood in exchange for the spurious securities of domination, appropriation, and escape. In the process, the most precarious aspects of human life are compressed into objectness. And thus our subjectivity, which exercises itself most fully in commitment, faith, hope, and love, is lost. With the evaporation of human risk, we experience the evanescence of freedom. The terrors of incompletion are denied, but in the denial our very selves are lost. And yet the pain remains, because no thing can ever deliver on its promises to frustrated personhood.

Christ would have us penetrate to the depths of our human personhood. He calls us to embrace and affirm our incompletion in acts of believing, trusting, and caring for ourselves, for each other, and for the God beyond us who completes us only in our freely given covenant. Our incompletion is indeed our poverty, but it is only in touching and living at the edge of this poverty that we may reach the fullness of our true power and destiny. Thus defenses against that poverty must be broken down. The Gospel sets before us the values and vision whereby such poverty can be lived and felt. They are values inalterably opposed to the values of

THE COMMODITY FORM	THE PERSONAL FORM
Value Grounded in Thinghood	*Value Grounded in Personhood*
Marketability of the person	Intrinsic value of persons
Production: worth as what you do	Worth as who you are
Consumption	Self-Gift
Thing-Knowledge	*Personal Knowledge*
Observation and description	Faith: self-consciousness and interiority
Measurement and control	Understanding and trust
Quality as quantity	Human quality as non-measurable
Emphasis on derived knowledge	Immediate experience
How-questions	Why-questions
Thing-Willing	*Personal-Willing*
Determinism	Limited freedom
Escape	Self-investment
Non-commitment	Covenant
Thing-Behavior	*Person-Behavior*
Violence:	Peace:
Domination	Acceptance of weakness
Manipulation	Respect of freedom
Retaliation	Forgiveness
Punishment	Healing
Defense	Defenselessness
Devaluation of Life	Exaltation of least person
Demand	Invitation
Competition	Sharing
Retention	Giving

THE COMMODITY FORM	**THE PERSONAL FORM**
Thing-Like Affectivity	***Personal Affectivity***
Sexuality as mechanics	Sexuality as sign of person
Body as machine	Body as temple— sacral presence
Fear/threat	Fear not
Non-commitment	Covenant—committed devotedness
Retention of self	Self-donation
Technique	Telos
Externality	Interiority
Replaceability	Uniqueness
Coolness	Tenderness
Hardness	Compassion
Accumulation	Detachment
Invulnerability	Vulnerability
Exchange	Prodigal love
Hedonism: immediate self-gratification	Generosity: suffering love
Thing-Reality	***Person-Reality***
Having	Being
What is	What we can be
Human skepticism	Faith and fidelity
Human paralysis and doubt	Hope and trust
Individual isolation	Love
Unfreedom as final condition	Freedom as final condition
Death	Life

the Commodity Form and its insistence upon our self-validating securities. They are linked, moreover, to specific models of human knowing, human willing, and human behavior, just as the values of the Commodity Form are linked to thing-knowledge, thing-willing, and thing-behavior. At each stage, we find the values of the Commodity Form and Christ in opposition. And underneath all opposition is the fundamental choice: Men and women are either revealed as things or revealed as persons. They are either secure but dead, or insecure but living and free.

I have tried to show how values, behavior, self-consciousness, and reality-perception are interwoven into entire fabrics. The Commodity Form and the Personal Form stand in opposition to each other on every level. They solicit from men and women, whether they are conscious of it or not, a final and totalized allegiance. Each presents itself as the ultimate explanatory principle, as the revelation of what we are and can be. Consequently, what we must do is first *face* this choice, consciously, and know that we are dealing with an option concerning what god to believe in.

In our culture, if we aspire to live in the Personal Form, especially as revealed in Christianity, we have to realize how the cultural gospel is not only an alternative to the Gospel of Jesus, but also a metaphysics of humanity, a philosophical worldview. As a worldview, as a theory of human realization, the cultural gospel perverts the fundamental exigencies of human identity into a denial of humanness and a denial of God. It offers a practically lived atheism and anti-humanism, insofar as it is an embodiment of the most fundamental of human sins: idolatry.

The power of this idolatry, of our original sinfulness, lies in its underlying rejection of our creaturehood, of our precarious created freedom. At the same time, it perverts the core of our identities as knowing and loving beings. To set up a god for ourselves more secure and less demanding than a God who would have us free and responsible, to set up a god-on-our-own-terms, a god who would fashion us not free but enslaved, is at the same time an act of self-alienation, a disenfranchisement of ourselves and of our true identities, and a rejection of love. It perverts our potentialities for knowing and loving into their opposites, and fragments our human community into an aggregate of isolated mini-divinities who claim to be the cause, source, and finality of being.

The Commodity Form, which serves as an undertow toward thingification, also channels our self-consciousness, valuing, and interpersonal behavior in the direction of dominance and self-aggrandizement. We are drawn into conflict among ourselves, and are led to believe that we will fulfill our insatiable longing for completion and self-realization on our own. If we can just collect enough, produce enough, or win enough, we will be god. We will have gotten rid of our painful incompletion. The paradox is that, as in every idolatry, we eventually entrap ourselves after the image and likeness of the idol—the thing we have created and trusted—the commodity: replaceable and obsolete, only quantifiably valuable, and bereft of freedom or qualitative growth. Thus the law of sin is indeed death. It is the death of our selves.

The Personal Form also beckons us to be Godlike, but by reaching down into the full meaning of our incompletion, not by running from it. Incompletion is one with being on-the-way, with being in process, with being a created freedom. It is one with temporal loving and choosing. It is one with the created project of collaborating in our own realization, not by self-aggrandizement and violence, but by yielding to who and what we are: free beings longing for the unconditional mystery of love.

Such "divinization" is effected only in freedom—in freely loving, believing, and trusting, in giving ourselves away and thereby finding ourselves. It is on this level that we discover and accept our destiny as being created in the image and likeness of a covenantal and freely creating God. The denial of our destiny as persons in this culture is nothing other than an ontological lie. The Commodity Form is the form of untruth, the sacred canopy of human obscurity and darkness, concealing us from ourselves and perpetuating our self-alienation. It is culturally legitimated pretense.

Perhaps now we can see that the Commodity Form and the Personal Form are at odds at their very foundations, as well as in the particularized opposition of the specific values we listed earlier. It should not come as a surprise that a follower of Jesus might find himself or herself to be an outsider in a culture dominated by the commodity. It should be no shame to feel different, even to feel a bit disjointed and out of place, in a civilization which divinizes the thing.

A Christian's values, if they have not been fully acculturated, are bound to be different. If we do not feel different, even embarrassingly different, something is wrong. Madison Avenueland, television, rock radio, advertising, will trigger constant reminders of our almost displaced existence. We will feel like strangers. The facts that life is cheapened, that retaliation and competition are conceived as ultimates, that familial consent and commitment seem alien, that armament and defense are so universally accepted, that fidelity in marriage seems strange—are thus not so dumbfounding as they might first appear.

I have heard Christian couples ask quizzically if *they* were the "weird" ones, so little does anything in this culture seem to agree with their deepest beliefs. They should not be distraught. They have merely come into contact with their faith as a lived, historical option. They have discovered that atheistic communism is not the greatest or only threat to their belief. It is lived atheism—whether capitalistic or communistic—which assaults their faith. And they have finally discovered the closeness of the danger—not in some different land, but in their own culture and its idolatrous belief system.

Such people, however, are not alone. Once having discovered the true issue of their lives, they will find out that there are countless other men and women who have made the same discovery. They will find that they can enter into communities of people who try to sustain their belief and aspirations in opposition to a powerful cultural gospel, people who attempt to come to grips with a culture they may in many ways love and desire to live within, but never ultimately succumb to. They will also discover how in their own belief as Christians they have a corporate life, a web of traditions, and a living basis of community that can support them in their choice for the gospel of Christ. It is this dimension which I will now investigate.

In doing so, I would like to mention again that I do not consider Catholic Christianity, or even Christianity, the only source of resistance to the Commodity Form. Too often Catholics and other Christians collaborate and compromise, rendering not only taxes but fidelity and conscience to Caesar. Too often I experience how the values and dogmas of the Commodity Form insinuate themselves into my own self-understanding and evaluation of persons. I am too aware of my own collaboration to deny the corporate collaboration of our churches.

Yet, the Catholic tradition and faith is the one which I know most intimately and which has both sustained and challenged me. I judge it to be the truest and most fruitful way to live in resistance to a commodified culture. Otherwise I would not attempt to live its faith or invite others to it. At the same time, I do not consider it to be the *sine qua non* of Truth itself.

Reversing the mountainpath analogy of our earliest reflections, I am convinced that if Christian, Jew, and Humanist penetrate to the depth of their commitments, longings, and beliefs, if they enter that depth with a painful honesty and an integrity open to the fullest mystery of their human personhood, they will find themselves, at the bottom of those depths, indelibly and eternally brothers and sisters.

CHAPTER TEN

LIVED CHRISTIANITY
IN AN IDOLATROUS CULTURE

If the revelation of Jesus Christ is an unequivocal testimony to the divine possibilities of men and women as open to mystery, to self-gift, and to covenant with God and other persons, then the spiritual community which bears his name could be expected to extend and embody that testimony of his life, death, and resurrection. Christ is God's response to humanity's calling out, an invitation to our fullest possibilities, a calling back to our essential vocation. Just as Christ's revelation to us was in terms of continuity and identification with the human family's truest identity, so also the presence of Christianity to culture must be one of such identification and invitation. The revelation of God is, in its deepest sense, the revelation of humanity. This should also be the foundational characteristic of those persons and communities who wish to embody such revelation in history.

Consequently, Christianity is at its heart a service of humanity and human fulfillment. As an historical and human reality, Christianity lives in and through cultures and is sustained by culture. To the extent, however, that a Christian church aligns itself with the pathological cultural values of appropriation and domination, it stands in need of self-purification from within—self-purification in the name of the very values it professes to believe in. A church can be unfaithful to itself and to the truth that it carries within it;

it is not exempt from idolatry or sin. The Book of Revelation makes this quite clear in addressing some of the early Christian communities:

Write to the angel of the church in Ephesus and say, ". . . I know all about you: how hard you work and how much you put up with. . . . Nevertheless, I have this complaint to make: you have less love now than you used to. . . ."

Write to the angel of the church in Smyrna and say, "Here is the message of the First and Last, trials you have had and how poor you are—though you are rich. . . . Do not be afraid of the sufferings that are coming to you. Even if you have to die, keep faithful, and I will give you the crown of life for your prize."

Write to the angel of the church in Sardis and say, ". . . I know all about you: how you are reputed to be alive and yet are dead. Wake up; revive what little you have left; it is dying fast!"

Write to the angel of the church in Philadelphia and say, "Here is the message of the holy and faithful one. . . . I know that though you are not very strong, you have kept my commandments and not disowned my name. . . . Because you have kept my commandment to endure trials, I will keep you safe in time of trial. . . . Soon I shall be with you. Hold firmly to what you already have, and let nobody take your prize away from you. . . ."

Write to the angel of the church in Laodicea and say, "Here is the message of the Amen, the faithful, the true witness, the ultimate source of God's creation; I know all about you; how you are neither cold nor hot. I wish you were one or the other, but since you are neither, but only lukewarm, I will spit you out of my mouth. You say to yourself, 'I am rich, I have made a fortune, and have everything I want,' never realizing that you are wretchedly and pitiably poor, and blind and naked too. . . . Look, I am standing at the door, knocking. If anyone of you hears me calling and opens the door, I will come in to share his meal, side by side with him. . . . If anyone has ears to hear, let him listen to what the Spirit is saying to the churches" [Rev. 2:1–3:22 passim].

I have used such a long citation because it is crucial at this point to recognize the ways in which a church can be idolatrous, enslaved, and unfaithful to its very calling. Thus our reflections here cannot be interpreted as a justification or legitimation of all the practices in the Christian churches. In fact, the evidence is ample and clear that many in the name of Christ have not preached his revelation but have prevented it.

One of the factors in such a deviation from a church's witness may well be the conflict between what has been called the "natural institution" and the "sect" models of Christian life. If Christianity is conceived as a natural institution, immersed in world and culture, its visibility and power in communicating Christ's message are enhanced; but there is the danger that in becoming "natural," acculturated, or secular, the actual message is itself distorted. In the sect model, the Christian community is not seen as a natural institution, and the purity of Christ's revelation is insisted upon; however, the sect has less social power, less influence in communication, and it is easily ignored or lost in the huge dimensions of other cultural institutions. The problem, then, is how to maintain one's identity while at the same time immersing oneself in the world by living in and through a culture. Some observations may be helpful in illustrating how internal infidelity can be faced and purified.

AGAINST THE IDOLS WITHIN

1. Self-Critique: Christianity is composed of social and cultural embodiments which are perspectival, incomplete, and unfinished. As a historical embodiment it consequently has the potential to become idolatrous or ideological and thus unfaithful to its vocation. It can become committed more to its own self-justified "sinlessness" and power than to the service of men and women and itself as loved sinners. Thus, the church has often read the Hebrew Scripture's prophets as a critique of Judaism or the world around, but not as a possible indictment of its own tendencies to idolatry and enslavement and oppression. In such a way it sets itself up beyond criticism and self-reflection in terms of its own values and scripture.

More dangerously, a church can become so acculturated and powerful as a natural institution that it finds itself in bondage to its own historicity. Thus we have seen painful and perverse identifications with the Holy Roman Empire, the Crusades, the Inquisition, the National Folk religion of the Third Reich, the aristocratic tendencies in Latin American Catholicism, and the co-option of "middle class" Christianity in the United States so often identifying God with country or even with free enterprise. In all these cases, the particular cultural milieu in which the Christian life is to be preached becomes the center and foundation of belief, rather than the life of Christ himself becoming that center and foundation. As a result, the church serves as a powerful source of cultural legitimation. It is identified with the interests of the culture and its most powerful institutions. As such, it can easily collaborate in the enslavement of men and women rather than in their liberation.

For example, the criteria of success which we found in the "American Fairy Tale" of production and consumption frequently appear in our culture as the measures of faith and religiosity. Achievement and wealth become endowed with redemptive, even salvific, power. Poverty and marginality, which should serve as signals of grace, are inevitably interpreted as the just deserts of "those lazy people who cannot take care of themselves." Thus the substantive teachings of Christ concerning justice, compassion, and generosity lose their clarity and power in a web of slickly spiritualized, but still racist and class-oriented, marketed myth.

Nonetheless, due to the very nature of faith, with its whole meaning rooted in a recognition of one's own poverty, Christianity has a perduring intrinsic basis for self-critique—of its own historical perspective, of its cultural embodiment, of its ideologizing, of its members. Faith must be lived or it is not real. It is the primary labor or "work" of the Christian, the Gospel of John says, to believe that we are the beneficiaries of a loving, unmerited redemptive act. The testing out of this faith is precisely whether it bears "fruit"—love of others, compassion, and equity. Thus, the only way to suppress the true Christian's sense of justice and compassion is to repress the very content of the Christian's faith.

It is true that at times such a repression may have been partially achieved; but never fully, else lived Christianity would have disappeared, there no longer being any fruit borne. But such fruit has always been borne—in individuals, in movements, in reforms, in mendicants, in men and women who have lived only to serve.

The impulse for self-critique and reform is felt by any believer who, conscious of his or her massive capacity for pretense, stands encountered by the Scripture. It is experienced by any Christian who has felt the distaste of being preached to about poverty and humility in the midst of power and pride, by any priest who has called his people to a life which he himself is too fearful or reluctant to live. It is exhibited in the endless questioning of children who feel the inconsistencies of our lives, and in the soaring feeling of adolescents who discover the Sermon on the Mount for the first time. The Gospel of Christ will always be ineffectually preached to any unjust social system if it does not first confront the church itself, and if, indeed, it is not a judgment and challenge for the individual believer.

2. *Interiority and Action:* The Christian faith is communicated by a witness and invitation which are encountered only through personal interaction and lived experience. Liberation, most fundamentally, is not a political, economic, or sociological phenomenon. It can be found—or accepted—only when we are made present to ourselves and our possibilities, only when we are in touch with our deepest humanity. Faith is not limited to class, not inaccessible to the poorest or the richest (although, as we have seen, it is more difficult to discover faith if we have entrusted ourselves to a spurious wealth covering up our interior and ontological poverty). At the same time we must recognize that liberation and faith are events that happen only in time, and as such are nourished or inhibited by certain kinds of economic, political, and social structures. Consequently, Christian action reaches out and extends itself to the environmental conditions of the culture—for there is no private realm which is not somehow touched and influenced by the public realm.

Social action is not the preserve of some special-interest group. It is an imperative of faith. This is true not only because of the content of the New Testament and the nature of the vocation to which Christ calls men and women; it is also true because there are social conditions which minimize the very possibility of experiencing love, hope, and faith. Destitution, degrading prisons, world hunger, and armament are affairs of spirituality. The human spirit is at stake, not "just" the human body.

Material poverty, as well as the addictions to consuming, accumulating, and winning, make the gospel difficult to speak and painful to hear. Thus, organized deliberations and resistance must be entertained, planned legislative change undertaken, and collaborative social service enacted by Christians themselves. The relationship of parts to totality holds. When a Christian couple works for peace, for food distribution, for legislative controls on advertising, they are enhancing the lived faith and joy of their children. When the same couple practices justice, fidelity, and compassion to each other and to their children, they are bringing about a change in their society.

3. *Moral Consistency:* In a given culture, there are many "language value-systems" and methodologies that can be used in the communication of a liberating faith. In a cultural ideology, however, the methods and languages become extremely restricted if a Christian is to retain any integrity in offering the gospel of Christ to others. The most blatant examples have been to use the power and fear tactics of a totalitarian state to make "conversions," or to torture people into conversion.

In American culture, the conflicts are far less blatant, even though they are significant. As we have seen, many of our socially accepted moral values and methods of action are founded upon a worldview and philosophy of the human person that is both anti-human and, *a fortiori*, anti-Christian. Principles of Christian activism, consequently, cannot embrace moral "language" or techniques which intrinsically violate the content of faith itself. Manipulation and deception, the Madison Avenue approach to religion, uses of dominance and intimidation, the appeal to violence—are all language methodologies which violate the content of Christian faith, whether they are practiced by a corporation, a revolutionary, a striker, or the pastor of a parish.

I have seen university students recoil from an "absolute Christian pacifist" who professed that he would kill Melvin Laird if he thought that that action would end the war in Vietnam. I have read Catholic "letters to the editor" in which convicts (like Gary

Gilmore before his execution by the state of Utah) were described as vermin and beasts to be "wiped out." If Christians are going to be selective in their application of gospel values (e.g., we can facilely articulate "just war" theories in which thousands of innocents will be killed, but we cannot tolerate anyone who might speak of a "just abortion"), they will have to honestly articulate the distinctions which enable them to approve certain forms of murder and not others.

Wholehearted consistency has often been lacking in the past, and it has made Christian witness ineffective and seemingly dishonest. It is a strange contradiction to condemn the values of materialism, and at the same time to measure a church member's love for God in terms of the money he or she contributes to the building of a church. These are all examples of the selective moralizing which has made Christian preaching seem deceitful and meaningless within the churches themselves.

4. Unity in Diverse Expression: It will be important to develop a viable philosophy of Christian action. Human activities, because they are placed in space and time, are necessarily partial, perspectival, and incomplete. Consequently they are intrinsically ambiguous in some way, somehow conditioned and limited. To accept ambiguity, to realize that the full range of Christ's revelation cannot be expressed in its entirety through historically conditioned action, is not a justification for compromise with death, aggression, or idolatry. Rather it is an admission of the human inadequacy of being in one space and time. No one of us can do all things, nor can all of us do the same things. What is needed, as a result, is a tolerance for the diversity of Christian actions, which unify and intersect in a common faith and longing but which ramify into a variety of methodologies and styles.

Opposition to armament or to abortion can be exercised in a legislature, in tax-resistance, in journalism, in jail, or in the pulpit. Resistance to racism or injustice can be practiced on a picket-line, in a classroom, through a newspaper, or within the intimacy of a home. The unity of the vision and faith is more important than the diversity of expressions. The interpenetration of diverse Christian approaches complements the singular incompleteness of each one. Unification of specific actions in a greater totality prevents the reduction of the partial methods into the culture as a totalizing ideology. It also prevents any one method, style, or action from assuming the role of *sine qua non* in Christian life and faith. At its doctrinal basis, Christianity is a religion of embodiment and incarnation. It must remain so in the realm of action as well. Some Christian radicals may live and talk as if they were somehow separated from their cultural ambient in some pure "ahistorical" state. But such is not the case in reality, nor is it desirable in terms of the very principle they profess. For their principle is a Person, a covenantal God embodied historically and culturally, and communicated through the limitations of language and temporality.

5. Freedom and Structure: The tendency to ever-intensified "pure" positions of Christian witness may be linked to the following phenomenon. On the part of many, the recognition of the pathological condition of social systems has led to an obsessive reaction to external structures, to the past, and to all institutional value-frames. For the most part, the disaffected have sought refuge either in the negation of all structure and values (historical embodiment) through utopianism, or in a flight from all structure through a noncommittal and debilitating tentativeness. Both alternatives seem naive and ineffective. The organic and evolutionary nature of change and growth is ignored in favor of anarchic structurelessness and an ahistorical romanticizing of revolution. Moreover, the mere polarization of forces, without a complement of understanding and love, cannot ever bring about the quantum leap into human realization. All the revolutionary inversions and permutations of the Commodity Form together cannot yield the Personal Form. Forms of perception and valuing can be apprehended only in terms of our own human historicity and its limits.

The second alternative—that of flight—is symptomatic of a hopelessness and a cynicism which emerge from our fear of "being burned" by fires of rapid change. In the actions of commitment, taking a moral stand or making life promises, structure is avoided because life is seen as too unsure and limits too confining. Young persons often talk of losing their "freedom" when they commit themselves to the structure of marriage. In actuality, they are operating out of a concept of freedom which makes any choice—self-limitation in history—impossible. You cannot choose without embracing structure. To insist on no structure is to exclude commitment. And that negates freedom. Thus, when freedom is mistakenly held to be exclusive of any structuring or stability in one's life, the whole self is never given with any passion to a person, an ideal, or even the future.

This paralysis in commitment, of course, enhances the hegemony of the Commodity Form. There is nothing real or true of itself, nothing worth living and dying for. The names for that condition are anomie and hopelessness.

It is a difficult and precarious undertaking to live a life of structured freedom. But it is the only struggle worthy of humans. We need to see and experience lived examples of men and women who have a third alternative to *(a)* pure structure, where people resist any change and openness to the future, where newness is feared and fled; and *(b)* pure freedom, which is an illusion of ultimate non-committalness, an escape from self-defining responsibility, a flight from the past and a dread of the future. Moreover, the living resolution of the freedom-structure dualism will assist us in terminating the other fruitless dualisms which hinder both Christian thought and practice.

World against heaven, action against prayer, technique against spirit, marriage against celibacy, initiative against authority, experimentation against tradition, conscience against law, community against individual—all of these polarizations result from a fragmentation of the vibrant totality of faith. Any choice between these polarities will be fruitless, for each pole is actually constituted and realized in its relationship to its so called opposite.

Heaven has its intelligibility *in* and gives intelligibility *to* this life. Action is short lived and fruitless without the centering of prayer, prayer is sterile without the fruit of the action. Spiritless technique and omni-directional enthusiasm are either impotent or deadly. Traditional authority lives in and is sustained only by experimentation and initiative. And morality is not the choice between conscience and law; it is the dialectical interrelatedness of both. Morality—committed human action in history—takes place only when the subjectivity of conscience collaborates with the objectivity of law and fact. In each of these spurious oppositions, the mutuality of freedom and structure is forgotten. In each of their resolutions, we will find people of faith and action who accept the delicate relationship between human structuring and freedom without rejecting either.

STANDING BEFORE THE IDOL

As we have already suggested, the Personal Form is not reducible to the Christian churches and the Christian churches are not exempt from the Commodity Form. In some ways, the Christian churches have helped generate and continue to support the imperialism of the commodity. Nonetheless, I have been maintaining that if a Christian were to honestly face the gospel of the commodity and the gospel of Christ, he or she would be driven to choose between ultimates, between final and authoritative interpretations of the meaning and purpose of human life.

The listing of the values of the Commodity Form does not necessarily lead to an increased burden of guilt for the Christian. Neither is the generating of some new program necessarily hoped for. Rather, of greatest importance is the attempt to focus our search for radical dependency on the redemptive power of God's love for us. Our reflections have been basically a method of being present to what, or whom, at rock bottom, we believe in, trust, and worship. Who or what saves us? Is it our securities, our accomplishments, our achievements, the rewards of culture and nation, our role as business persons, priests, professionals, even our own fidelity? Or is it the prodigally loving act of redemption in the reality of Jesus Christ? Is it his way, his truth, his life that we subscribe to and believe in or is it the catechetics of capitalism?

If we say Jesus Christ, then we are called by him to a life of simplicity, a life without racism or vengeance, a life of compassion and trust, a sharing of our goods, a consciousness of and attention to the world's poor, and a committed covenant in faith, hope, and love. In a culture increasingly demanding the thingification of human life, we are called to struggle for the personalization of the universe. In a world made ever more mechanical, threatening, and alien to personhood, we are called to render reality benevolent.

True moral conflicts arise, however, when, in our well-founded and sane recognition that things, production, consumption, technical reason, even competition, cannot and should not be ignored in the building of human life, we accept these values as ultimates. In our witnessing to the world, in our participation in "culture-building," the world has come to be too much with us. We Christians compromise with the "powers that be," with wealth, hedonism, nationalism, and economic ideology. We become too comfortable with Caesar.

Having faced the dominant gospel of our culture and compared it to the gospel of Christ, we should arrive at a growing recognition that our relation to this culture can be only as people apart. Christianity at rock bottom radically conflicts with American culture, even subverts it. The last thing that Christians need is to become more secularized.

In recent years, attempts of Catholics to release themselves from the Roman and ecclesiastical appurtenances of the past have introduced the danger of being too fully identified with the cultural imperatives of the present. Thus the easy talk of secular cities, religious hedonism, Christian fulfillment, and sacred national pride have seduced many of us into yet another form of cultural support rather than cultural critique. This is the very thing that has happened in more traditional "acculturated" lifestyles of Christians—only the traps were in the form of superfluous and conspicuous wealth, a legitimation of social classes and pacification of the poor, a predominant association with cultural and national power brokers, and a refusal to take stands against social inequity or armament programs.

In a culture of lived atheism and the enthroned commodity—whether in its traditional forms or in its pseudo-liberated surrogates—the practicing Christian should look like a Martian. He or she will never feel fully at home in the commodity kingdom. If the Christian does feel at home, something is drastically wrong.

To feel like a freak in an alienating society, however, is not to be sundered from the people of that culture. The deepest longings of men and women, even in our culture, have not been so efficiently repressed that the desire for truth has been extinguished. All humans yet long for something to believe in, Buick notwithstanding. They yet desire community—even if it is a group of friends who, as Camus suggested, spend their lives telling each other that they are not God. Persons still yearn to live lives of integrity. They yet yearn for mystery that is not magical but personal. Service still beckons them. They feel the suffocation of a closed materialistic universe, and their pain surfaces in a variety of searches for something and someone beyond. They bridle at the enforced skepticism about their most primal hopes. They have felt the bankruptcy of the secular gospel and its divinization of the market.

In this context the situation of contemporary Christianity is not entirely unlike that of the very early church—huddled in frail expectancy, newly aware of its own sinfulness and capacity for self-betrayal, painfully conscious of its inadequacy. Even in the context of the writings concerning the apostolic and pentecostal church, we can sense the atmosphere of divisiveness which had threatened the community, the threat of rupture between particularists and universalists, between Peter and Paul, between Jew and Gentile. And this community felt the ever present possibility of being swallowed up by the powerful cultural forces of Eastern religions and the Roman empire.

In so many ways, Christian men and women today are huddled together in their basic longing, in their experience of powerlessness, in their sense of sinful searching for false power and the security of idols. They have experienced divisiveness within the Church, within religious orders, within the realms of cult, moral practice, dogma, and life style. And they feel oppressed by the present Roman empire, the lived atheism of the Commodity Form, in which life, human sexuality, labor, love, and human dignity itself are subject to alienation. The new forms of slavery, the onslaught of relativism, skepticism, and selfishness are bewilderingly omnipresent.

Ten years ago the problem appeared almost insurmountable—not because of the power of the Commodity Form, but because of the fissures within Christianity itself. Conservatives clung to the past, to militarism and to nationalized faith, as relentlessly as radicals baptized mindless change, revolution, and hedonism. Today, however, after probing to the depth of our own poverty as humans, and yielding to it and opening ourselves to the possibility of rebirth, Christians seem to have discovered a new interest in Scripture, a commitment to interior depth through prayer and retreats, and an openness to communitarian movements. In some instances they have witnessed a rebirth of the parish as the focus for the strengthening of a lived, rather than nominal, Christianity. In other cases, Christians are experiencing a regenerative return to evangelical radicalism—leading not to American chauvinism and displays of wealth, but to gospel simplicity and pacifism. Out of the individual and shared acceptance of sinfulness and poverty has grown the common experience of standing in radical covenantal relationship in Christ. It is a relationship sustained by his promised Spirit of peace, forgiveness, strength, and fearlessness, aware that it is consecrated not to the world, but to the truth preached in faith and lived in trust. It is Jesus—not any privileged group, not even any Christian group—who has conquered the world of darkness and death.

The foundations of Christian unity are so profound, and so desperately needed in this fragmented culture, and the stakes are so high, that it would be a tragedy for both faith and society if Christians were to be paralyzed by their differences and embrace spiritual isolationism. United in the essential faith of one Lord, one covenant, one history, a shared sinfulness, a shared promise, and a mutual commitment to the kingdom preached by Christ, Christians can call each other not to their differing partialities, but to the only totality worth living and dying for: freedom in Jesus Christ.

If Christians are able to give themselves in wholeheartedness to the life and promise revealed in the person of Christ, if they are willing to be encountered, "judged," and called to a consistent living of the gospel, then they will be able to stand before the world, before any culture, and speak their variety of tongues. They will prophesy, heal, interpret, and live a life of freedom in faith, hope, and love. They will stand against darkness, against idolatry, and against slavery, as they embody living resistance to the claims of the Commodity Form. Their resistance will be rooted not in their own self-righteousness or posture of sinlessness, but in the truth which they carry in faith. Recognizing the deepest values which they share with all men and women in their most profound longings, conscious of their poverty and dependence upon God, they can bring the Personal Form into fuller realization. What the powers of culture have deemed impossible, they will live.

The reception of the revelation of Christ, however, as well as its profession to the culture, takes place in the contexts of history and of relationship. Consequently, the ideals to which Christians find themselves called will have to be sustained in the arenas of common history and societal life. This is most important today, since it is so frequently on the corporate level of life that the power of the Commodity Form exercises its greatest influence on individuals. In order to more fully respond to the invitation of the Personal Form, Christians must consider the practices of their own tradition as well as possible models for communitarian and corporate embodiment of what they believe.

CHAPTER ELEVEN

CHRISTIAN PRACTICE
IN THE PERSONAL FORM

COMMUNITY:
RESPONSE TO CULTURAL ISOLATIONISM

A life of faith and of hope and of love rises in contradiction to the values of the Commodity Form in our culture. Faith, hope, and love are the three human activities deemed most impossible by the cognitive and behavioral standards of commodity consciousness. In Catholic tradition, one believes that these three human acts are "theological virtues"—the highest exercise of our human personhood, wherein we participate in the very life of God. Thus, not surprisingly, the anti-humanism of our culture is at the same time a lived atheism.

Lived belief, the lived practice of these theological virtues, must conflict with the received conditioning of our social, political, and theoretical systems. It is this conflict, as well as the facts that we are intrinsically social beings, that we are intrinsically inter-subjective, and that the revelation of God is in and through a community or a people, which lead us to a recognition of our need for community. Our faith vision is received only in terms of our history and psycho-social development; if it is to be nurtured and purified and sustained, it will also have to be in terms of our historicity and sociality.

116

Traditional religious communities (which we will briefly discuss later in this chapter) have been, despite the lapses, enduring focuses of shared communitarian faith and witness aspiring to the revelation of Jesus Christ. But today there are a number of newer emphases upon Christian community life: from a growing sense of a priest-brotherhood found in *Jesu Caritas* communities, to the Focolare movement, to the Jean Vanier communities of the handicapped, to counter-cultural Christian communities modeled after the Catholic Worker. The Cursillo movement and Christian Life Communities continue to develop, with regularly shared prayer and faith sessions, ongoing communication, and longer-range commitments. The Charismatic Renewal movement also emphasizes the communal dimension of praying, of healing (memories, physical and psychological suffering) in the context of community, of greater emphasis upon continuing personal contact and support within chosen or parish-located groups. The Marriage Encounter movement likewise stresses the communal sharing of faith, prayer, and some goods, and the mutual support of families in their commitment. The Sojourners, the New Jerusalem, and peace communities of activists all offer witness to faith, and service to men and women. Inner-city pastoral and justice groups undertake regular communal prayer and meetings of shared faith. Groups of informally gathered married couples study and discuss their vocations. Christian professional groups cluster in families for the confirming of life, ideals, hope, and plans. These are all examples of the movement among Christian people for a new sense of corporateness and communality.

All of these groupings are based on the discovery that a Christian, in the face of our culture's dwarfing and isolating of the individual, must turn to a community of shared life-experience which both fosters committed faith and enables the individual to criticize and challenge the programming of the culture. The most effective means by which both goals are achieved is in a communally shared Christian life.

Physical growth, both individual and social, is cellular; the same principle applies to the life of faith. Christian cell-communities should be formed which will call forth *(a)* an internal fidelity of the members to a life of prayer, shared faith, and mutual encouragement and correction, *(b)* an internal critique of personal and community actions, apostolates, and goals in the light of faith, *(c)* an opening of their shared life of faith to others by hospitality and encouragement in the Christian life, and *(d)* external critique and planning with respect to changing the social and environmental conditions that inhibit personal integrity and growth within the local community, the city, the nation, and the Church.

In each of these areas, the community will have to be present to itself: as fundamentally Christian in commitment and orientation; as counter-cultural in its advocacy of the Personal Form; as non-competitive in its encouraging, sustaining, and challenging; as corporately conscious of its most fundamental choices in faith and specific life options; as unified in its orientation to service, freedom, and the work of justice.

Such a communitarian life demands a commitment of time, energy, and sacrifice. Its mutual support system cannot take place outside of a commonly recognized commitment of persons to each other in the name of their shared vision. A community of this kind must be *(a)* consciously choiceful, *(b)* explicitly committed to and willing to be called to the life of the Gospels, *(c)* open to change through the authentic living-out of its principles, and willing to be challenged to fuller Christian praxis, and *(d)* prepared to confront the patterns of the Commodity Form—injustice, manipulation, domination, dishonesty, escape—not only as they appear in the culture at large but also *as they surface within the group itself.*

In the process of sharing and deepening a living corporate faith, a Christian community will recognize that if it is not possible for a group of mutually committed men and women to struggle honestly with their own propensities to injustice, competition, and non-responsibility, they will hardly be justified in challenging those same patterns in the society at large which they criticize. They will realize that there is something fundamentally unjust in indicting other people or institutions for failing to do what they themselves refuse to undertake. This is the meaning of internal *and* external critique.

One's personal life, as well as the life of the community in which one lives, has social and political dimensions. That is true both in the sense that the communitarian life is in itself a stance and a witness against the Commodity Form, and in the sense that the same behaviors of domination and violence in international, national, and urban groups are potentially operative in a group of men and women who come together to foster and deepen their own Christian lives. If they are able to face and purify the patterns of injustice in their lives together, they will be able to bring greater compassion as well as insight to those patterns which are found at broader social and political levels.

PRAYER: FORMATION OF A CHRISTIAN IDENTITY

When a Christian community acknowledges its own brokenness and poverty, and also brings its vision of the Personal Form to society, it will need to call upon resources other than its own. The basic resource, of course, is faith in Jesus Christ as the revelation of God and humanity, and through Christ, his community in history—a freely entered church. The ecclesiastical dimensions of dogma, faith and morals, cultic practice, and universalism are crucial aspects of the individual and communal search for self-identity and continuity.

It seems to me, from my own experience as well as from the history of many communal movements in the church, that any Catholic community which is to survive cannot test its relationship to the Catholic community of believers in much more than one area of dogma, morality, cult, or universality without seriously jeopardizing its identity as Catholic as well as its potential for speaking to its fellow believers out of a *commonly* embraced union of hearts. While it is a painstaking and risk-laden enterprise to call into question or challenge traditions in *one* area—e.g., cultic formalism, the ministry of women in the church, the particularities of moral practice in social life or sexual life, the investigation of the meaning of dogma or Scripture's inspiration, or the possibilities of indigenization—the strain of unity becomes considerably heightened if more than one of these areas are challenged. This is not so much a question of critique as it is one of identity. For example, it would seem that the depth and long-lastingness of Dorothy Day's witness to her fellow Catholics in the area of social justice and gospel simplicity are directly proportional to her unequivocal orthodoxy in the other areas of dogma, cult, and universality. To the extent that her continuity with the praxis of Catholicism has been unimpeachable, the fruit of that faith borne in loving service and pacifism has often become irresistible to the mature Catholic conscience.

The power of the charismatic movement, likewise, and its striking impact on the Catholic church in introducing a radically different form of personal and corporate prayer, is clearly linked to its continuity with the universal and historical church as well as with the Sacred Scriptures.

But to be a community which calls into question celibacy, a male clergy, permanent commitment in marriage, the trinitarian formula, transubstantiation, traditional prayer, and the church's social positions, all at once, is to be a community with no solid identification in itself, no clear lines of continuity with the historical community of believers, and no foundation for witnessing to *commonly shared* values and beliefs. Any hoped-for prophetic action or witness is lost because the shared universe of signs, values, and beliefs has been diminished and dissipated into relativism and subjectivism. And this relativizing of universal faith, in turn, abets the cultural forces that form our identity and claim our allegiance.

If any relationship, any person, any community is to grow, it will *develop out of its totality* and its historical continuity. At a certain point, when too many factors of continuity are displaced or lost, the person or relationship will experience not growth, but fragmentation and eventual dissolution. Consequently, as it understands and appropriates its own development, it will be important for a community as well as a person to have means whereby a centering of identity and continuity with history can be supported.

In this context of centering and grounding one's historical identity, there are two special means and traditions practiced in the Catholic church which are worthy of extended discussion and consideration. These are the dimensions of prayer and of the sacramental life; and we will consider them, for our purposes here, precisely in the light of their relationship to the Commodity Form, the gospel of culture, and the rooting of identity within change.

Prayer is a social and political act. It cannot be considered otherwise when we reflect upon the societal and political revelation of human life that we find in the Commodity Form. We have seen its underlying themes of idolatry, the denial of covenant, the flight from intimacy and interiority, the insistence upon control and manipulation, and the absence of freedom in faith, hope, and love. Prayer, on the other hand, is most fundamentally a covenantal relationship with another person—God—and it partakes of all the risks, struggles, joys, and darknesses that attach to any personal intimacy.

As an act of interiority, of entering into solitude, prayer demands the major effort of extricating oneself from the patterns of behavior which have become normative in commodity consciousness. Centering ourselves in prayer is an exercise in being present to our identity and purpose as persons, in locating the desires of our being which cannot be fulfilled by the false promises of the thing. The very act of being consciously present to ourselves is a mammoth undertaking in resistance to facile externalization, to cultural pressure, and to social expectation. This is a crucial reason why prayer can be so difficult—especially if we are people under the thrall of cultural imperialism. It feels just too strange even to locate ourselves as persons. There is no empirical payoff, no immediate guarantees of success, no way to measure or control, no way to evaluate competitively.

Silent solitude is filled with risk. It lacks pragmatics. It is hopelessly unmarketable. The centering of prayer is ultimately an exercise in honesty, in getting in touch with our needfulness and poverty so shrilly denied by commercialism and materialism. It is an exercise in self-revelation rather than self-deception. Prayer is an assault upon the fraudulence of mere roles, of social and cultural pretense, of the idols we cling to and are enslaved by. As such, it carries with it all the existential terror of any act of intimacy with another person. Afraid of being "found out," we avoid the intimacy. We cannot speak to another person from the depth of our being. Thus it is not only prayer to God which is found to be so impossible; any prayerful communion with another person seems equally inaccessible.

Yet we long for personal communion. Somehow we do long to be found out. To be seen as we are—to be accepted as we are. This is what takes place in the intimacy of prayer. We discover that the

God who is revealed to us in Jesus Christ has "found us out" already and not rejected us. Thus the news at the bottom of our identity is not despicable and desolate. It is good news. The declaration of our poverty, of our dependent needfulness, of our incapacity to save ourselves through idolatry, of our ontological incompleteness, is not a shameful discovery, but a discovery of our being loved for what we actually are. We need not hide our fragility in order to be loved.

This is the message of prayer. It is the message of any personal love—achieved not by a few minutes' method, or a crash course, or a renewed physical glamour, but by the risks of placing faith and hope in another person. It is a life task. It is a commitment. We disengage ourselves from the universe of values and possibility legislated by the demands of culture.

The moments of prayer are (1) a freely-entered presence to one's self, to one's deepest longings, and to the personal God one professes to believe in—involving, at the first step, acts of faith, hope, and acceptance of oneself as one is; (2) a recognition and truthful acceptance of one's poverty and needfulness in the presence of God, and a crying out of one's ontological contingency; (3) a listening to God's response (such a listening is possible only when one accepts one's own incompleteness) not only in Scripture but also in the movements within oneself; and (4) a giving thanks and returning of one's self to God when one recognizes that one is loved into being and loved for one's very being.

Consequently, the whole process of prayer—its quieting, its truth, its centering in being rather than in having—is characterized by profoundly counter-cultural activities. Contrasted to commodity living, prayer seems inaccessible, impossible, remote. It is beyond our power (of course) and control, and hence unmanageably fearful. What is most intimate to us is felt as most alien and frightening. And so we stay away—from our selves, from intimacy. Thus prayer is not only a counter-cultural act. It is a reappropriation of our personhood and identity. It is a de-alienation, a decommodification of our very lives.

Corporate prayer exhibits similar structure, even though it is experienced at a different depth. Charismatic prayer manifests similar patterns of acknowledging poverty, of healing the perverse forms of idolatry, of admitting and accepting creatureliness, and of breaking into praise founded upon radical trust, acceptance, and the experience of saving love. Shared prayer, when it comes from openness rather than from obsessiveness, talkativeness, competition, or quantification, exercises our openness in faith before the other. It is a declaration of intimacy not only with God, but with the others in whose presence we reveal our poverty and aspiration. It overcomes the isolation and separateness that cultural values impose. It demands a recognition of our common frailty, breaking through the covering masks of self-subsistence, independence, and self-justifying idols which construe being loved as both threatening and unnecessary.

Perhaps we can see, then, the political and social *content* of prayer. Prayer is not somehow a realm separate from or untouched by the cultural milieu. In fact, it is precisely the cultural, the social (and psychological) dimension of prayer which makes it seem so impossible to undertake. But just as entering prayer is a breaking of bondage to the cultural gospel, so also the fruit of prayer is an empowering of the person in freedom, discipline, and commitment to stand before the gods of culture and yet to live otherwise. Prayer thus yields one of the most dramatic and sustaining forces for centering our identity for authentic social action and for long-term social commitment.

SACRAMENTALITY: FORMING THE LIFE OF PERSONS

Among the traditions and practice of the Catholic church, the sacramental system has played a crucial role in calling Christians to themselves. Even in their most formal historical expressions, the sacraments, with their use of Scripture, have served as continual sources of interior renewal and self-criticism, and of the development of deeply committed men and women. It is as if the power of the sacraments has been greater than any of the corporate deviations from Christ's life, greater than the destructive possibilities of full inculturation, greater than the blandishments of magic or the blandness which comes with the loss of the transcendent and the mysterious. The sacraments have been a constant focus of the dialectical relationship between the transcendent and the immanent, between the God "beyond history" and the God of space and time.

With the arrival of Christian secularism's fashionableness, much of the sacramental system has been called into question. This acculturated devaluation of the sacraments has been compounded by the turbulence of much needed changes during the past decade. In the past, the heart of sacramentalism had surely often been neglected in an over-concentration upon externals; but advocates of change have just as often depended merely upon modified formalities as the hallmark of truth and growth, and in the process the full power of sacramental life has often remained untapped.

Nonetheless, the sustaining influence of the sacraments persists. It can be discovered in the countless elderly men and women who are able to see the faith of their ancestors in the faith of the young, and in the young who have come to discover and embrace not only their renewal, but the best and deepest of their past. For my purposes here, I wish only to highlight the social and cultural dimensions of sacramental life; but I believe that this highlighting will quite probably touch upon what is the very identity and power of sacramentality.

Sacramentalization is an elevation, an exalting and celebration of the most intimately human aspects of our lives. Sacraments retrieve and make holy the critical moments of growth and human development. They celebrate and embrace the truly human. Each sacrament is a centering, a recovering of humanity to itself through the inviting power of a God who pronounces what is deepest in human persons as something irreplaceably good. Thus while all of the sacraments are a remembering and making present of the life of God in the life of humans, they are also a revelation of, a remembrance of, humanity for itself.

Personhood, commitment, and covenant are the hallmarks of sacramentality. So also is memory. The sacraments are personal and corporate affirmations of the Personal Form. They are rememberings of who we are: rememberings of our humanity, of our frailty and needfulness, of our covenants, of our power for commitment, of our social nature, of our creatureliness, of our marvelous destiny. Every key concept in this paragraph is a concept of the Personal Form. Centering, commitment, personhood, faith, hope, love, needfulness, and human fulfillment as persons are missing from among the conceptual categories of the Commodity Form. In fact it is my suspicion that it has been the Commodity Form's prominence in advanced industrial societies that has in great part led to the devaluation of the sacramental life among Catholics—not because sacramental life itself is under attack, but because the value of human personhood has been reduced to the commodity and its criteria of what is real and valuable.

While the Commodity Form dulls us into forgetting our truest identity and so separates us into isolated competing units, the Personal Form engages the memory of our personhood and so establishes our unity in that personhood. The sacraments are rememberings: rememberings of our creaturehood, in birth, sickness, and death; rememberings of our history, of our being saved, of our being called; rememberings of our covenantal life choice; rememberings of the precious *present* which we take for granted and so often forget. Since the opposite of remembering is not only forgetfulness but dismemberment, the sacramental life is also a celebration of our *unity* in covenant, and our destiny as persons called forth by God. A sacrament *re-members* us, puts us back together, heals our individual and corporate fragmentation. As such, sacraments are crucial, even in the specific forms they take, for our effort to embody the universality of our personhood in a way that transcends culture, countries, class, society, and temporal history.

Infant baptism, as it is presently practiced, is a celebration of birth, of community, of life. It is the corporate invitation extended by a community of faith to a new human being—not in order to predetermine his or her life, but in the consciousness that the stakes of life and choice are too high for indifference. Thus the community wants and claims the child for its life of covenant, freedom, and faith.

At the same time the community calls itself and its families to a renewed commitment, in covenant and promise to the child and his or her future. Baptism is a corporate and familial recognition of our human poverty—not as something to be escaped, but as something to be embraced in the recognition that we are chosen precisely in our frail humanity for the self-transcending life of knowing and loving. As a corporate act, as an affirmation of commitment and covenant, as a recognition of human dignity and mystery, it is profoundly counter-cultural.

Just as the Commodity Form of life touches the full range of our experience as men and women, just as it is a "form of being" and a "formation system" for acculturating persons throughout their lives, so also Baptism is the initiation of a person's entire experience of faith in God. Baptism is the beginning of our corporate and social formation in the realm of the Personal. It suggests, moreover, how the sacramental life itself is a Personal "formational" system that challenges cultural formation, in life-crises, in service and covenant, in our ways of reconciliation, even in our manner of dying.

Baptism is the family's and the community's commitment to a "counter-cultivation" of our individual development. A culture *cultivates* us—educates, tills, and tends us. A culture is also a *cult*, a religious value and behavioral system that fosters and nurtures us, that can easily claim and engulf us in a world/life vision. To baptize our children, then, is in a sense culturally subversive: it is a commitment to cultivate and give a cultic vision to our youngest loved ones, which is a radical alternative to the social-economic "cultivation system" that is the Commodity Form. It is also, and more significantly, the incorporation of the child into the very life of a triune covenantal, personal God.

The Sacrament of Confirmation while not historically instituted and practiced as such, can be considered to be a celebration of mature commitment after a period of years of formation in Christian practice. It is a commission, in the form of a covenantal profession that our vocation—our being "called forth"—is through the Spirit, who establishes us in the truth of Christ which the world itself may not only misunderstand but may even condemn. Just as Jesus in the Gospel of John returns to the Jordan, the source of his baptism, when during the feast of the reconsecration of the Temple he experiences the resistance of the world and its rejection, so also our adult rededication is made in the face of our knowledge of the cultural gospel and its blandishments.

Reconsecrating ourselves to the task of fashioning our lives in the manner of Jesus' living and dying, we follow his Spirit in our life-choice of service rather than domination, healing rather than violence, and redemptive love rather than hate. In reciprocity, our community of faith and resistance "missions" us to the praxis of Christian life and strengthens us with the very power of our covenanting God.

From this point of view, we can see how Confirmation could be fruitfully regarded as the sacrament of the mature single life—surely a life-choice quite distinguished from Marriage and Orders, even though those more specified life-choices may be embraced in later years. In our culture, which so often reduces marriage to a rite of passage into adulthood, Confirmation in the Christian community more deeply identifies the patterns and commitment of a freely chosen Christian life of sexual integrity, generous service, and personal fidelity.

The sacraments of Orders and Marriage (both of which we will discuss more fully below) are further covenantal celebrations of life-commitments, as ministers to the Christian community and as spouses in the shared intimacy of mutual sanctification. At the heart of each of these sacraments is promise-keeping—the recognition that the only irreplaceable gift, to the world or to an individual, is the gift of one's self.

Within this self-donation is the equally counter-cultural value of permanence in commitment. Stability of life-forms and intimate relationships, constancy of moral values and promises, are both powerful supports for the formation of men and women of conscience and solid identity. Instability and impermanence, certainly, are most conducive to the passive acceptance of external power, environmental control, and social engineering.

Penance, or the Sacrament of Reconciliation, is the remembering of our need to forgive and to be forgiven, the acknowledgement of our sinfulness, the owning of our desire to heal the fissures in our lives, our practices, our relationships. It is a compelling sacrament, one most difficult for contemporary people because of the cultural pressures not to recognize our ontological poverty, not to face our contingency, not to give up the idols we grip for false security.

The Sacrament of Reconciliation is especially hard, not really because of the embarrassment of self-revelation to a "mere human," but because the objective honesty which such a revelation requires is painfully real to the penitent. It is inter-subjective; my sinfulness becomes communally and socially known to another person. Such a socially acknowledged need for forgiveness and repentance is boldly contrary to our privatized inclinations.

Indeed, it has to be admitted by church people that the failures of past confessional practice, the compulsions and obsessiveness associated with the Sacrament of Penance ("religious scruples"), the frequently induced fear and lack of compassion, the distorted focusing of all morality upon sex, and the scandalous inadequacies of priests have often diminished the healing power of this sacrament. But the tragedy is that in a time when the actions of self-revelation, acceptance, honesty, and forgiveness are so desperately needed, it is precisely this Sacrament which is least practiced. Its full reconciling force will never be experienced unless we ask for and grant forgiveness for past mistakes and sins and proceed to see its social, political, and cultural significance for the present. To confess one's sins is not only the beginning of a change of heart: it is a liberation from servitude to cultural pretense.

The forgiveness of sins, surely founded upon the saving love of God in its ultimate sense, is essentially a *communal* reality. One of the reasons confession has been so ineffectual in the past is no doubt the neglect of this fact. The "unrepentant penitents" could continue to hate, to be racist, to be unjust and unreformed, as long as there was no social claim made upon their consciences and privatized sins of selfishness, pride, and impatience went unchallenged. Any attempt to give pragmatic reality (by suggesting a "penance" of corporal works of mercy or forgiving someone or telling the offended person about the lie or calumny) would have been met with powerful resistance. Much of the "rote" character of sin-telling was precisely an act of avoidance. Much of the selection of confessors was made precisely on the basis that there would be no socially objective acknowledgement and challenge of sinfulness. My own school, twenty-five years ago, had two favorite priests: one who couldn't hear and one who couldn't speak. Deadly serious as to guilt and compulsion, people were often completely repressive of the possibility for true repentance and change. So it will be with all exercises of penitence that fail to take seriously the communal and social nature of faith and sacrament.

The Sacrament of the Sick is the ultimate victory over the gods and idols and fears of our culture. In a civilization that systematically represses the actuality and implication of our creaturehood, that covers over the natural dimensions of dying with technique, circumlocution, and the empty smiles of Sunday morning religious hucksterism, this sacrament admits that death is real, but proclaims that it is not the last word.

We affirm faith's power over sickness and mortality. We say that there is more to us than material monuments and things, that our indestructibility is intimately related to our covenants, and to our capacities for faith, hope, and love. We affirm the efficacy of faith not only in the context of a loving eternal providence, but even in our physical and temporal dimensions, as in God's power we heal our interior sufferings and often our physical distress.

The Sacrament of the Sick stands directly in confrontation with our dominant myths and values. It is a reliance in faith that we are loved creatures. It is a final embrace of our humanity, an entry into the very dying of Christ with trusting abandonment. Our "last" sacrament, then, stares even death in the face and empowers us to be fearless.

I mention the Eucharist last because it is the sacrament most fully embodying the Christian life, the Personal Form, our ways of communal resistance, and the act of remembering. The very structure of the Eucharist recapitulates the other sacraments in so many ways. It relives the life of Jesus. It embodies our corporate mission as a people of service. First of all, in the Eucharist we acknowledge that the only way we can come into each other's presence and the presence of God is as sinners. A great divestment of our egoisms and our claims to self-righteousness is the precise moment of entry into the mystery of God and communal life. It is an act of unilateral disarmament, a declaration of peace to be recapitulated throughout the entire eucharistic celebration. It is a request for mercy.

The Eucharist is, secondly, an act of listening. It is uncommon in our society that a group of people would open themselves to be called and judged by the word of God. Not only is the listening posture uncharacteristic of a civilization compelled to make noise and distracting clatter, but the willingness to be moved and changed by the testimony of something other than profit, self-interest, or pragmatics is truly remarkable.

In the sacrament of Christ's redemptive sacrifice, we also celebrate and consecrate our own gifts. We identify our lives, our labors, our passions, and our joys with the body, blood, history, and person of Jesus. It is an attempt to reconfirm our choice of loving and life-giving service, as we reproduce in ourselves not only the manner of Jesus' death and resurrection, but also the very substance of Jesus' reality as food for his brothers and sisters.

Recalling our history and salvation, becoming mindful of our own need for the healing action of God in our lives, remembering our sinfulness and reliance on a covenantal God, and making Jesus our own life and sustenance, we give thanks. Seeing the face of our God in food that sustains us in our poverty, we are sent forth to minister to our brothers and sisters in poverty, through whose faces, again, we will encounter the living God. The "sacrament of the poor" reminds us of the poor.

This is not theory; this is reality. In my own experience as a priest, I have found two people who receive the body and blood of Christ as no others. They are Teresa of Calcutta and Jean Vanier. There is only one other time in their lives that they can be seen to respond to the world with the same rapt intensity: when they are receiving a poor person into their lives, or when they are receiving you as a guest.

The Sacrament of the Eucharist is the celebration of the redemptive act of God in human history. It necessarily engages the personal realm in us—unless we are able to repress its essentially social content. In that case it will not change us, it will not transform us. It will only have the effect it has had on two people who have walked to the same Mass for fifteen years, and during the same fifteen years have refused to speak to each other.

The Sacrament of the Eucharist is corporate, interior, covenantal, and celebrative in its exercise of freedom. This sacrament elevates the commonplace, the symbolic, and the communal to the very life of our Trinitarian—interpersonal, social—God. It is an exaltation of our humanity, because in the Eucharist we are involved in the life and gift of Jesus as the unifying focus of God and humanity.

Each sacrament, which is a participation in the life of Jesus-God-and-human, is a revelation of the personhood of God in which our own personhood partakes and is ultimately realized. Each sacrament belies and resists the gospel of the commodity. Each, even the Sacrament of Sick, confirms and embraces life in the midst of a civilization that has enthroned dead things. Each declares independence from and liberation from the chains of culture and its confined universe. Each sacrament is an act of freedom and covenant, in a society that declares both impossible. Each is exercised communally in a nation where community is dead. Each embodies faith, hope, and love in a world of minimalized risk and marginalized care.

Thus the sacraments are at the same time the engagement of human persons and divine Persons in covenantal relationship. They are prayer. They are politics.

MARRIAGE AND CELIBACY: COUNTER-CULTURAL LIFE CHOICES

Two dominant aspects of the gospel of commodity, as we have seen, are the erosion of permanent commitment and the thingification of human sexuality. While the media supposedly celebrate sexual liberation, sex in the media has no linkage with the full human person or human covenant. In this cultural ambience it becomes evident that the sexual life of Christians has considerable importance not only in their personal adherence to the gospel of Jesus, but also in terms of witnessing to human personhood.

The only intimacy recognized in the Commodity Form is physical proximity. Knowledge of the other person as a person is painfully absent for many couples who enter marriage even though they may have considerable physical knowledge of each other. With the heightened hedonism of our culture, moreover, the pains of suffering and sacrifice are considered as impenetrable evils to be avoided at all cost. The continued intimacy of a shared life which is open to new life, however, is one which necessarily entails the suffering of growth and of daily dying to immediate gratification, to the satisfaction of one's clamoring ego, and to one's defenses against self-revelation. It is precisely in the fires of this struggle for love and commitment that marriages fall apart.

The high incidence of divorce cannot be separated from the dominant values of our society. The breakdown of familial covenant is part and parcel of the commodified universe, with its values of competition, hedonism, non-involvement, non-risk, loss of faith, and hopelessness. Many, even the most idealistic, enter the life choice of marriage with skepticism about their love, with paralyzing fears that it cannot last, and with lurking suspicions that they cannot give themselves unconditionally. And the very conditions and reservations they bring to the commitment actually determine the instability of it.

It is my belief that the institution of marriage (as well as the institutions which support its indissolubility against intense cultural propagandizing in the media) is one of the last bases for resistance to the Commodity Form. The family provides a primary sphere of human life where the deepest experiences of fidelity, of trust in other persons, of self-acceptance, of growth in intimacy, can occur and can offer data that belie the absolutes of capitalism. When families are broken apart, the incursion of the Commodity Form into the life of the child is even more far-reaching than otherwise. For a family-less child, the *only* data about life and love comes from media, social pressure, and cultural expectations. If covenantal marriage dissolves in this culture, the Personal Form may well disappear.

Part of the devaluation of the institution of marriage derives from the devaluation of human sexuality. The continually increasing incidence of pre-covenantal sexual intercourse among a majority of young people serves to separate the fullest expression of bodily intimacy from the interiority of total commitment and personal intimacy. Sexual intimacy receives both its intelligibility and its deepest eroticism from the intimacy of persons. Divorced from personal intimacy and the commitment upon which it is founded, sex itself becomes a social and personal lie. It is transformed into an object of immediate short-range gratification, in avoidance of the self-investment appropriate to a life-long covenant and profound self-revelation. It is again quantity, often in different combinations and different packaging, which is substituted for the more fundamental longings of the human person.

In a culture which portrays life-commitment as impossible and undesirable, which inhibits the flowering of true intimacy, which deems a suffering love and sacrifice to be negative values, men and women who enter into a personal covenant by mature and free consent are taking a radical stance.

In an environment that intimidates persons who face risks made in freedom, that has reduced human affectivity to aggression, domination, and control, a life of marriage will be both terrifying and, at the same time, one of the most profound sources of liberation from the dialectic of domination and appropriation. It is a learning how to die, to accept one's finitude, to accept another person, to be stretched toward unconditional love, to truly share not only one's goods and gifts but one's poverty and life-grace.

In a society dedicated to "holding on to" everything, a life of marriage entered in the Personal Form is a schooling in how to give oneself away.

Sexuality and commitment as they are perceived through the Commodity Form provide the context wherein the issue of celibacy may be most fruitfully discussed. It is not surprising that in a culture which systematically attacks the covenant of marriage, the devaluation of other forms of chastity (I mean an integration of one's sexuality with one's whole personhood and life commitment) prevails. Chastity is impractical, out of date, undesirable.

The mutually sustaining forms of chastity in marriage and in the single life are yet to be fully investigated—especially the ways in which the struggles of celibate love are enhanced and nourished by the witness of faithful married love, and how the purifications and "dyings" of married love are complemented and sustained by men and women who live lives of celibate love. Both forms of chastity witness to the human condition and its full promise—one under the form of committed intimacy to another person and the risk of openness to new life, the other in a dimension of non-possessive loving and non-privatized care that is considered to be unacceptable foolishness in the canons of acculturated sexuality.

A celibate who lives a warm and affective life of intimacy which is not reducible to genitality, and a life of hope which is not reducible to the blood of offspring, says by this life-choice that human happiness, tenderness, compassion, and passion are made possible by our very humanness and a caring life of faith and hope. Such a life, of course, is more difficult in the doing than in the saying. It is true that there is great power in the witness of celibate love, in its implicit affirmation that one's personal choice has no intelligibility without eschatological faith and hope in Jesus Christ. In our culture especially, people have found it dumbfounding that someone might find human intimacy and compassion while foregoing physical fatherhood or motherhood and choosing to love without lover, spouse, or sexual gratification.

But it is also true that many celibates fail to give the ideal witness of the celibate life. The pains of relinquishment can be frequent and intense. The physical incompletions felt in intimacy without genital orientation or expression are filled with difficulties, purifications, and an aching vacuum close to the bottom of one's physical life. Care and carefulness are difficult to express in an integral way, and the sequential struggles found in a life of celibacy are as trying as the struggles in married love. There has been failure—not only in the high incidence of men and women who have rationalized their vowed public commitment in compromise and deceit, not only in those who have tried to change their commitment in openness and integrity, but also in the more culturally acceptable (and dangerous) forms of infidelity to celibate love. So often celibates have merely displaced their affective life rather than transforming it. Love and care are directed to things, possessions, games, professionalism, achievement, and the collection of trifles. A loss of tenderness and compassion, of affection and passion often seems to accompany the vowed celibate life. The concentration of all of one's moral sensitivity in moralistic sexual preoccupations may also be a by-product of a celibacy not grounded in love of Christ and of other human persons.

All of these risks and dangers, however, are worth taking, not only because of the intrinsic value that a life of celibate love can embody, but also and especially in the light of our culture's sexual gospel. Chastity, both in the marital and celibate forms, stands as a rare testimonial to human integrity, to the symbolic and actual importance of being embodied selves, to the preeminence of personhood and covenantal life. In a hedonistic culture, moreover, chastity is a most effective concrete critique of fulfillment through immediate gratification. It is a living refutation of the reduction of persons to either machines or animals, to progeny or to pleasure. The contradiction is well known. This is why sexual integrity is under such relentless attack in advanced Western societies, why it has to be explained away as deviance, repression, or frustration. It is a scandal to Madison Avenue, Hollywood, and the halls of academe and Rockdom. Yet it exists, and as a phenomenon within our culture, the life of married or celibate chastity can be a most subversive lived force today. It is truly counter-cultural.

The blind acceptance of the Commodity Form is especially evident in the realm of sexuality. Somehow we are led to believe that there is a sexual liberation going on—as if, mysteriously, human affectivity and sexuality were exempt from the hegemony of the thing. But if we look at sexuality and its mechanized commodification in our culture with any degree of honesty, we will see that this is not the case. The so-called sexual freedom is the affective erotic expression of the dominant economic and philosophical "reality" preached by our cultural gospel.

The wisdom of our capitalistic society in its marketing of sexuality and immediate gratification would have us believe that sexual integrity and commitment, chastity and marital fidelity, are something dreamed up by celibates in Rome hoping to impede our gratification and increase their control over us. The truth is, there is indeed a great deal of control over and manipulation of our sexuality, but it is not exercised by clerics. It is exercised by the market and the thing. There are societies and civilizations which never heard of Roman Curia but which have insisted upon the importance of sexual integrity. But they have not been in the grips of a commodified universe and its overwhelming promotional power.

THE VOWED LIFE IN COMMUNITY: RESISTANCE TO INCULTURATION

In recent years most religious orders have been puzzled and frightened by the drop-off in the numbers of people applying for admittance. The only communities which seem to have grown are either those which have been heavily emphasizing traditional values, or those which, like Mother Teresa's Missionaries of Charity, have also made the investment of themselves in a life of un-equivocal witness to the gospel and service to the poor. In both of these cases there is an interesting phenomenon which is not too often looked at: each presents to a young person a *real alternative* to the gospel of the "World," a real possibility of living in a way not dictated by the lords of culture. In the case of sheer conservative emphases, the motivation could of course simply be the superficial distinctiveness of religious uniform, a rigorous rule, and formal singularity. It may also be a mere flight from the world and even from one's self. But it is quite clear that a way of life *different* from *passive acculturation* is sought. Most of the orders and congregations which have lost great numbers, or have even been disbanded, seem to have been the ones that have also foundered in finding their new identity in response to the call of the church for renewal: in too many cases, change has been merely a move to further acculturation, secularism, and the adoption of cultural values.

I believe there are many alternatives to the superficial conservatism on one hand, and the panicky trendiness on the other. One powerful and often overlooked possibility is in the rediscovery of the religious life as a counter-cultural force. Men and women religious are called to be special Christian activists, who, by their subversive mode of life, invite other men and women to question the obsessions that dominate their social world and prevent them from being open to their own full potentiality as persons. "Religious" can live in the world, certainly, in continuity with the truly human, rooting themselves beneath and within various human projects—economic, educative, social, political, and ecclesiastical—with the aim of liberating themselves and others for mobilization into deeper Christian life. None the less, by the quality and intensity of their prayer and shared communal lives, they will witness to the fact that the human condition is not reducible to social and political projects. Their lives will clearly point to values that transcend the limits of nation, race, class, or ideology, and that sustain their commitment to each human effort they undertake. A covenant with and in Christ remains central to their vows, but the very *evangelical* nature of their commitments leads them to be culturally radical.

In their openness to one another, in their fidelity to the Word of God, in their renunciation of dominating power—even though isolation might be less demanding, infidelity less precarious, and power more immediately satisfying—religious have the opportunity to bear unambiguous witness to *faith*, founded in the God who invites. They choose *obedience* to God's calling forth of their personhood, expressing it in fidelity to their Christian tradition, to their life promise, and to their common struggles.

In their relinquishment of private property and its accumulation, in their rejection of self-aggrandizement and all forms of psychological or economic possessiveness—even though extensive property is the aspiration of our culture, and aggrandizement the promise of material fulfillment—religious have the opportunity to witness unambiguously to *hope*, grounded in the God who shares. They choose to be *poor* by letting go of final reliance upon possessions and by a trusting abandonment to the Lord.

In the risky gift of their lives and the vulnerability of their self-divestment in compassion—even though self-withholding seems the guarantee of security, and dispassionate coolness the model of cultural isolation—religious have the opportunity to bear unambiguous witness to *love* grounded in the God who gives. They choose to be single-mindedly *chaste* in the passionate gift of their whole selves without reservation.

We can see, then, how the traditional vows of poverty, chastity, and obedience are not only expressions of a life of faith, hope, and love, not only fundamental commitments to human freedom, but also relentlessly counter-cultural stances in the three crucial areas of human action. It will be well to elaborate on this.

In the area of property, capitalist culture offers human fulfillment under the guise of infinite accumulation, appropriation, and competitive self-enhancement. The vow of poverty is a stance taken in freedom not against property *per se*, but against security and fulfillment in property. It is not a negation of things, it is an affirmation of their proper ordering in human relations: persons always before property. Men and women cannot be fulfilled, saved, or made happy by the production or accumulation of commodities. They are fulfilled only when they relinquish their idols, only when they see things as *expressions*, and servants of personhood. The vow of poverty emphasizes detachment, simplicity, sharing, and a celebration of the goods of the earth. In each emphasis, the vow then embodies a value-stand against cultural dogma. At the same time, it is also a solid foundation for social activism, rooted in the conviction that the human person is primary in ethical, political, and economic life; thence follow the moral imperatives of equity, the fair distribution of wealth, the obligation to help the poor and dispossessed, and the desirability of communitarianism. The vow of poverty is the theoretical and practical controlling limit on our relation to property and things.

Religious life demands it as a bulwark of its fidelity and promise. But our culture needs it even more desperately.

The second major area of human interaction is in the issue of power. We have seen how this issue is resolved by the cultural gospel, with its emphasis upon *laissez faire* marketing and morality, upon isolation and individualism, upon domination, control, and competition. The vow of obedience professes that isolation and egocentrism, as well as the violence that arises from them, will not rule one's life or one's community. It is a purification of the ego's demands for self-sufficiency. Obedience is a commitment to resolve human struggles not through domination, but through openness to the other and a yielding of one's "non-negotiable demands." Obedience is the willingness to be named, to be called, and to be held responsible as an interdependent social being.

The final crucial area of the counter-cultural stance of the religious vows is human affectivity. Not only is this area repressed in the Commodity Form; it is also displaced, by the reduction of human sexuality to mechanics and disspirited coupling. Musculature displaces passion. Love is a production, a making, a making it. It is a performance and a drive to legitimation. Commitment is evaded, as we have seen, and the purifications of our desires and affections never take place. Rather, they are channeled into the seductions of escape, violence, and manipulation. The vow of chastity, on the other hand, professes human interiority and the trans-cultural, trans-temporal sacredness of the human body. Letting go of the immortality of blood it affirms the eternality of Love. It is an exercise of free disengagement from cultural imperatives; it is a declaration of independence from the devaluation not only of sexuality, but of personhood itself.

In each of these basic areas—power, property, and affectivity— the person who lives the vowed life finds himself or herself in radical opposition to the values of the culture. In each area, moreover, we have a social and political programmatic, an alternative model of human interaction and growth, a foundational model for entering and changing the cultural ambient. Sharing. The primacy of persons over property. Responsibility in a mutually accepted interdependence. Human loving. The elevation of sexuality to a human act.

So many men and women who live the traditional religious life of the vows do not make such connections. Traditionalist groups fail to draw any relationship between the life they profess to live and its socio-political impact. They often present themselves as political quietists with personal and corporate financial security.

More reformed groups have succeeded only in passing themselves off as accomplished "men and women of the world." What special gift do they have to offer? They are not perceived as a challenge to or hope for the desperation of our society. And often, uninformed by prayer, asceticism, or passionate spirit, they perceive themselves as secularists with little to live or say. In both cases, the powerful content of the three vows is neither perceived nor practiced.

In this instance, religious men and women fail to touch the energetic sources of their vocation. And it is precisely this misconnection which underlies the ineffectual changes that have been attempted. Only when we see ourselves as social and cultural beings who have chosen a gospel other than the one offered by the culture itself can we discover our full vigorous potentialities and make the changes that are incumbent upon us. Only then can we see the necessity for a life of integrity in our sexual lives, a life of authentic sharing, simplicity, and detachment in our use of things, and a life of true responsibility and commitment in obedience.

We are witnessing, perhaps now more than ever, an increasing demand for a more explicit presence of Christian communities and their living of the life of the gospels and evangelical counsels. The need is even more pressing when situated in a civilization that grows continuously more materialistic, individualistic, and consumption-oriented, more technologically trapped, more mechanistic in its affectivity, and more fragmented in its long-range life commitments.

If my reading of our culture is correct, the last thing desirable for religious people is an easy identification with such a culture. The last thing needed is another milieu-culture Christian or milieu-culture community. Christianity indeed must be lived in space and time within cultures—but always beyond the culture, transcending it and transforming it, and if necessary working against its values as a counter-cultural force. The life of the traditional vows is an attempt at an admittedly limited "unambiguous

statement" about the fulfillment of persons in non-appropri-
ation, in a love which is not reducible to genitality or mechanistic
sexuality, and in a committed life of mutually shared risk and
openness to the other.

We presently experience a growing awareness, on the part of
many young persons, of the desirability of and necessity for a
shared community of prayer, vision, support, and resistance to
the idols of capitalism. Many young people are recognizing that
their faith, hope, and love have to be made explicit and embodied
in community consciousness and action. Yet these people find little of the direction and leadership they seek. They look for the
encouragement of lived witness and invitation, but the lived witness is too often ambivalent, too often like the culture itself; and
the invitations are too often hidden, too often timid.

At the same time, a considerable number of men and women
who have embraced the life of traditional vows and community
are experiencing a call to a personal and communal rebirth as
Christians. They desire to have their faith and vows more radicalized and centrally focused upon the Gospels and the person of
Christ. They experience this call not so much as a judgment upon
the past as a judgment upon their own future.

Moreover, there is a growing need for mediation in the Church
and in society, due to increasing polarization, incapacity for tolerance, and the instability of men and women in their life promises.
It has to be questioned whether the present structures of the parish and religious houses are truly capable of meeting these polarizations and challenges. Perhaps a more intense communal life of
prayer, celebration, and service is the most appropriate response.
But there is little leadership available and few viable models of
community life are offered. In response to such a situation, it
would be well to consider whether traditional communities could
see their mission as providing models for corporate living and
sharing which are less culturally ambiguous and more open to the
larger church around them.

Many communities of religious in their training live in large
buildings (even though they might be divided into smaller sub-
groups) that tend to separate their members from other people,
because of environmental necessity or for the sake of efficiency or
academic efficacy. Many undesirable possibilities emerge: iso-

lated personal lives, irresponsible and dishonest attitudes towards poverty, anonymous security and abundance, unresponsiveness to communal needs or excessive waste, and assumption of leisure-class values and aspirations, with ignorance of critical social issues and decisions (racial prejudice, abortion, militarism, media exploitation, penal reform, urban decay). These are often the by-products of isolation, suffocating comfort, and false security.

After the completion of religious formation a person often tends to find self-definition in terms of an institution, a school, or a professional task. Sharing frequently takes place on this level alone—students, classes, projects. Sharing of faith, doubts, communal strategy, decision-making, mutual encouragement, and correction become privatized and increasingly infrequent. What is neglected, because it is taken for granted and rarely made explicit, is the fact that faith and the life of vows rooted in Christ are the only sustaining bases of corporate identity and personal meaning.

Moreover, the institutional frames themselves tend to separate religious men and women from other people. A religious faculty as a community of service and faith rarely shares its life with the lay faculty even to the simple extent of sharing meals with them, Eucharistic or other. Rarely are outsiders regularly invited to pray with the religious community. The houses take on the appearance of closed fortresses; at least that is the way they are frequently—albeit sometimes unjustly—perceived. Community life can become so closed as never to have a basis for sharing lived faith with fellow professionals, students, friends, or even members within the community. What is shared is knowledge, professional competence, even ministerial powers—but rarely the intimacy of a life lived in faith and hope.

In some unfortunate moves toward smaller communities, none of the difficulties above are really transcended; rather they are transposed merely into another smaller, more private, more secularized, more comfortable environment. What we lack in these cases—as in our dying large communities—is a model of communal life that emerges from a cultural and social understanding of the meaning of the vows in a lived atheistic culture. What we lack is a vision of community life which is apostolic in the very offering to society of an alternative way of living and being together. What we lack is an insight into the dialectical relationship between faith and society.

Religious communities, in their effort to renew themselves, miss the power of their own traditions and the vows when they search for ways to make life more amenable and luxurious, or more isolated and rigidly formal, or more cozy and undemanding. An understanding of how the Commodity Form has insinuated itself into both the conservative and the modern models of community might serve to unleash the full potential of communities of men and women who openly testify to a personal and corporate living out of the gospel of Jesus Christ. Too often religious life has been and remains a testimonial to affluence, financial survival, isolation, and individualism—the hallmarks of the Commodity Form way of life. It need not be that way. But it will be otherwise only if we so choose—newly conscious of the cultural and social context of lived faith.

RESPONDING WITHIN THE TOTALITY

When we consider the vast range of the Commodity Form's influence in our lives, whether it be in national policy, in our media, or even in its forming of our personal experience, the sense of its totalized presence can overwhelm us. Where to begin? How can one start to resist and not have one's beginnings be some futile, fragmentary gesture? The variety of the ways of expressing commitment to the Personal Form might appear to be too much to handle. A resolution to this threatening sense of paralysis about so many problems and so many possible responses can be found only when we once again understand and apply the "principle of totality"—the fact that our personal lives, our faith, our labor, are all intimately related to social, political, and economic reality.

Our understanding of the all-encompassing struggle between Christ and idolatry as competing *total worldviews* which claim our allegiance should qualify all of the concrete choices and particular options before us. It is our final commitment in faith which vivifies and gives meaning to the partialities of limited decisions and conditioned expressions of that commitment.

The totality—a life of faith in Christ—lives in and is sustained by the particularities of diverse parts; and the parts receive their life and meaning by their relationship to the totality which is at the center of our lives. This, ultimately, is the meaning of the Mystical Body, a doctrine which helps us articulate how the Personal Form can be embodied and enacted in our different lives and labors. We all have distinct gifts and life-choices; they are a coherent organic whole by virtue of the common Spirit we share. The particularities of how we resist the Commodity Form are necessarily different for each of us; but the universality of our common allegiance to the Personal Form in faith unites us.

As a summary, I will attempt to simply suggest how one might integrate one's life, embodying concretely the unity of faith and justice and at the same time maintaining a vision of the whole. The example I give will be that of a middle-class Catholic mother of three, but the schematic pattern is applicable to men and women religious—teachers, administrators, spiritual guides—to professional lay persons, to blue-collar workers, to old and young.

1. Personal Life Choice and Centering: First it is important for her to be in touch with the depth of her life-choice and concrete situation. Prayer will be crucial, as a regular method of centering her life, of bringing order to the constant demands and tasks that fashion a home and young family. Without this centering in faith the totality will never be made conscious. She will be lost in particulars which become duties exacted of her rather than expressions of love and choice. Without centering, she will be unable to see how the compassion, affection, care, and structuring she provides her children are important social acts, are furtherances of justice, and are profound methods of resisting the Commodity Form. She will be unable to see how the crucible and joys of intimacy with husband and children are actually the testing and living out of the revelation of Christ. She will miss seeing how the purification of her needs and demands are actually worked out in relationship, and as such are related to the suffering and victory of Christ.

Her centering in prayer is a declaration of independence from the thousands of culturally created pressures in her head pushing her around with threats and fear. Prayer liberates her from our culture's criteria of success. Daily centering is an "enabling" activity, whereby she becomes once again conscious of the irreplaceable present and extricates herself from endless tapes about the past and endless rehearsals of the future. She repossesses her life and mind and feelings. Prayer brings her in touch with her deepest identity, her most basic desires and hope, her poverty and her promise. This centering with her relationships of intimacy will be foundational in any human expression of the Personal Form in Christ. It will also be crucial to her resistance to the Commodity Form. If this does not occur in her life, all other procedures and tactics will be worthless.

2. Style of Life: This woman's interior dispositions and commitments, her most basic desires, must be *embodied* in concrete practice. The fruit of the experience of authentic prayer is action at the most immediate level of experience, one's style of living. Everything need not be done at once, but something must be done as the embodied expression of her commitment and desire. She will not let television be a surrogate life for herself or a substitute intimacy for her children. She will live more simply—release herself from the addiction to buying and consuming, cut back on the superfluous meat-eating which injures health and ultimately deprives the poor. She will treat Christmas less commercially and competitively. She will consume less alcohol, seek less after the appurtenances of comfort. No one of these expressions will be a *sine qua non* as an act of resistance to the Commodity Form, but some expressions must be made. Concrete practice, even if it is a simple thing, reminds us of who we are and what we choose. These changes in her style of life will enhance her ability to pray, will open her up to more people, and will heighten her concern for justice.

3. Community: As a married woman she will find it important to enter into collaboration with other people, to share her family's strengths and struggles, to communicate her faith, to encourage and be confirmed in her choice. This will involve not only the formal relationship to a parish community, but also a more thoughtful interaction with other couples at the deeper level of faith for mutual challenge and support.

Taking a stand against the imperatives of competition and individualism of our culture, her participation in some kind of community structure will be embodied by regular commitments to prayer, discussion, celebration, and social service. This experience of community will break through the cultural myth of isolationism which inhibits our capacity to form deep communal relationship.

4. Social Justice—General Consciousness, Particular Action: A fourth factor in integrating the Personal Form in this one woman's life will be an ongoing education in issues of social justice, even if her family commitment makes much activism impossible. The consciousness of the relationship between faith and justice will not only open her to the emerging issues of equity and liberation, it will also give her personal and family life a social and political content. Connections have to be made—not only among the wide diversity of issues, but between social issues and her familial commitment—as resistance to the cultural gospel. Raising a family will be seen as an act of justice as well as an act of faith.

A merely "general understanding," however, will not sufficiently embody her societal commitments. In addition, it will be important for her to give some portion of her time and energy to at least one movement for justice—to serve as a conduit for others, to be knowledgeable of a particular issue's implications, and to take part in legislative lobbying, group organization, or demonstrations, for example. Commitment to a particular issue, as well as the power and resourcefulness of her commitment, will depend on her capacity to integrate and concretize her "partiality" to the wide variety of struggles against the commodification of men and women. Thus, critical consciousness of the spectrum of social problems and how they are related to the underlying Commodity Form will sustain and be sustained by her investment of time in one specific exemplification of the person-commodity conflict.

5. The Gift of the Dispossessed: A married family woman will meet constant opportunities to be in touch with the impoverishments of human life—in the utter dependence of her young children, the ever constant purifications of yielding their future to hope and trust, the sufferings and truth of intimacy. At the same time, however, it will be valuable for her to have some kind of continuing and regular contact with the very poor, the dying, the lonely, the handicapped—not organizational or support work, but immediate contact.

The impoverished, as painful as their struggles are, have an unequalled power to educate us to our pretenses, our fears, and the rejection of our humanity. The handicapped often have no pretenses to cling to, and in their openness and necessary acceptance of their poverty they can disarm our greatest fears. Thus, this woman will learn to see herself in the poor, encountering her own impoverishment, her own aging, fear, and sense of abandonedness. In allowing her to be a part of their lives, the marginalized will engage and call forth from her greater fearlessness and love. They will empower her for fuller truth and compassion.

The struggles for social justice, the necessity for political change, the penetration of prayer into her life will take their most profound hold upon her only when she is in touch with her true poverty as human by identifying with those who have come to be called the dispossessed. Her initial fear and anxiety will dissolve when she yields to their presence, faces her humanity, and surrenders to her own neediness. She will find her commitments purified and deepened, her family life enriched. Her life of prayer will become more real. Her style of living will change profoundly.

More schematically, then, if we wish to embody our covenants and exercise our awareness of faith in relationship to culture, we must integrate all the varying levels of our experience. Just as the Commodity Form makes its way into each arena of our lives—in our loss of personal focus, in our isolation from each other, in our personal manners of consuming and living, in the broad structural realities of social injustice, and in our repression of our consciousness of the marginalized poor—so the Personal Form must live in and permeate each experiential arena. Just one area will not be enough. Prayer alone will not work, unless it is tested in relationship and its fruit is borne in the works of justice and mercy. Community alone suffocates in self-interest if it is not sustained by individualized life-commitment, prayer, and the outreach to service. Style-of-life changes without a sense for justice and an ongoing contact with the poor are ineffectual and ultimately self-defeating. Tithing one's time for the marginal, for it to be an authentic and lasting commitment, can be maintained only by a life of prayer, community life, and the intimacy of centering and resting in the truth of prayer. The project of holiness in society is just as dialectical as the power of social and personal disintegration.

All areas of our lives interpenetrate, live in and through each other, and actualize the life of the totality. Such is the mysticism of the Body. The integration of the parts enables the totality of faith to be concretized and sustained in our daily lives. Such an integration is the only enabling resistance to the idols of capitalism. It is also the only enabling response to the Gospel of Christ.

The Commodity Form of existence makes claims upon our lives through the systemic interpenetration of every area of our experience: the loss of solitude and personal identity, the dissolution of community and commitment, the insensitivity to the multifaceted occurrences of injustice, the insinuation of consumerism into our very manner of living, and the repression of our consciousness of the poor.

We must allow the gospel of Jesus to do the same, for the claim of God upon our hearts and lives is as systemic as the claim of idolatry.

The life of Jesus is not only that wherein we are saved, not only that by which we are instructed; it is also the very *way*, the very methodology, of Christian praxis.

In the early stages of Jesus' public life, as the Gospel of Luke presents it, we can discover how Jesus makes his own response to the call of God and the challenge of the world. After having fully committed himself to partaking in our humanity through his baptism, Jesus is led under the power of the Spirit into the desert (the poverty of solitude and personal prayer). He then emerges radically changed in his manner of living, having resisted the temptations to the pleasurable, the spectacular, and the powerful (style of life). He goes back to Galilee to announce the good news to the poor and set the downtrodden free (laboring for justice) before he undertakes a life of ministering and healing (tithing to the marginal and the "least"). Weary, he calls friends to himself to share in the apostolic undertaking of the kingdom (community life).

Thus the interpenetration of all these aspects of personal life is not only a sound tactic for resisting cultural idolatry. It is not only a method for incorporating the gospel into our lives. It is the way of Jesus who is the Way.

CHAPTER TWELVE

CONCLUSION: REVOLUTIONARY HOLINESS

The practice of Christianity has too often been isolated from its social and cultural context. To the extent that it has been so isolated, faith has been ineffective—both in the impact that it has had on the lives of Christians and in the power of its witness to the culture in which it exists. On one hand, Christians have been too uncritical of the ways in which the economic system and the political structure have influenced and even distorted Christian values. On the other hand, Christians have been unimaginatively dualistic in their understanding of how their faith might be of social and cultural importance.

Even in so-called "Christian" cultures like ours, the operative values and modes of perception have often been virulently anti-Christian and anti-human while people of belief persisted in pretending that such a social and political environment had nothing to do with faith. In its most distressing instances, organized Christianity has actually served to legitimate worldviews and political systems whose values are diametrically opposed to the message of Christ as found in the Scriptures. With the excuse that they were merely rendering unto Caesar what was Caesar's, Christians have not infrequently rendered unto him their consciences, their life purposes, their hopes, and even their children. The problem has been most intensified in those cases where Christian churches have been closely identified with worldly or cultural power. The legitimation of that power soon displaced fidelity to the gospel of Christ as the foundation and guide of the Christian life.

Today, the situation of Christians in American culture is paradoxical: although the culture is nominally Christian, the values of our society are appearing as more and more antithetical to those of the gospel. Reading the signs of the times can jar us into seeing the striking oppositions between cultural wisdom and Christian wisdom. It is my belief that the Commodity Form claims such ultimacy and takes so powerful a hold over our consciousness that we are obliged to make a choice of final allegiance between contradictory accounts of how humans might be served and saved.

A critical awareness of the Commodity Form and its pervasiveness in our values and perceptions is the first condition of such a choice. It is only when we face up to the fact that there are fundamentally opposite readings of the human situation beckoning our allegiance that we can face the choice that is upon us. This consciousness, moreover, enables us to see the pattern of values that underlies a wide diversity of issues which so often tend to separate and isolate us—values usually based upon prejudice, special interest, or selective application of principle.

Only when such consciousness is operative can a Christian perceive that racism, abortion, militarism, are not questions of mere politics. They are questions concerning faith in God and humanity. It is not a matter of personal preference or privatized morality that a person resist the legitimation of capital punishment and abortion, or protest the selling of armaments and Saturday night specials; it is a question of how that person views human nature, its dignity, and purpose. There is a Christian view. And it is unalterably hostile to the dominant view of the Commodity Form.

Our purpose here has not been to prove that capitalism is essentially contradictory to the message of Christ. Even though that could indeed be the case, we have been more interested in showing how capitalism, if it is not subjected to standards of a value system or vision of humanity outside of its own criteria for truth, value, usefulness, and success, is inherently destructive of humanity, and *a fortiori* systematically opposed to Christianity. For, in the absence of any other belief system than itself, capitalism will fabricate its tyrannical idols and subject men and women to a bondage and spiritual destitution as devastating as any totalitarianism.

Christians have much to learn from Marx and many Marxists. Their passion for equality and human dignity, their sense of moral outrage at the alienation and subjugation of human beings, and their commitment to a change in unjust social orders, are all instructive. These are the very qualities that some Christians tend to ignore—even though these qualities and values are at the basis of Christianity itself.

If Christians had the Marxist sense of critique, if they had a Marxist awareness of how the economic order is intrinsically related to the entire social and religious fabric of a society, if they had the wholehearted dedication to the betterment of humanity that many Marxists exhibit, their Christianity would take a more profound hold on their lives as well as on the world. Their Christianity would be lived and real, rather than nominal and superficial. There would also be less complaint that the only problem with Christianity is that it hasn't been tried.

Marxists, on the other hand, indeed, have much to learn from Christians, and everything to learn from Christ. Class analysis and rigid state structure underwrite violence, destruction, and a metaphysics of fear. The terror of men and women who live in a totalitarian regime is undeniable. The Commodity Form and its world of advertising propaganda is perfectly mirrored in personality cult, group tyranny, and the relentless programming of children.

At the center of Marxism is a gaping hole. It is absence of spirit. There is little of compassion and hope. There is a lack of faith in the resilience and freedom of men and women. And most damaging of all, there are ultimately provided no good reasons for persons to be free and alive. People are expendable, because, again, there are no controlling limits to ideology. Having no transcultural, trans-statist values grounded in the human person, men and women are the sacrificial offerings to the idol of the idea. Only in those Marxist countries where there is a thriving culture-transcending faith is the power of resistance felt and the dignity of the individual affirmed against totalitarian pressure.

Christians, when they abandon the questions of justice and

hunger, of poverty and militarism, to socialists, liberals, and Marxists, do as great a disservice to their own identity as to the human community. Quietism and passivity not only perpetuate injustices committed against humanity, they also undercut the central fact of Christ's life and message. Jesus called to the attention of the disciples of John that he is recognized and preached precisely *in* the actions of justice, compassion, and human liberation. Christ *identified himself* with the face of the poor, the dispossessed, the hungry, and the imprisoned. To exclude them and their oppressed condition from the content of the Christian faith is to exclude its founder and Lord.

Excluding the social, political, and cultural content from Christian faith debilitates the church in other ways. First, having left the questions of justice to social activists, agitators, and Communists, many Christians paradoxically see the movements of justice and liberation as the work of atheistic Communism and the devil. This is a profound perversion of their own religion, sadly compounded by the identification of all the evils in the world with communism.

Thus externalizing evil, the church suffers a second debilitation in the absence of interior self-criticism. Critics within the church are seen, and often perceive themselves, as the enemy; thus they often leave the church or are forced to leave it. Any hope for an increased fidelity to the revelation of Jesus Christ is short-circuited when the church denies its own sinfulness and need for conversion. Only the "others" have to be converted. And we forget that having denied our sinfulness, we may also ignore the beckoning of the Lord who came to call sinners.

Finally, a further debilitating aspect of the faith/society dualism is that the church fails in its mission to its own culture. The values of a culture are somehow written off as being "out there," as being neutral to faith and spirit; thus the most powerful impediments to faith, embodied in the Commodity Form and the Idols of Capitalism, go unchallenged. And not only are they unchallenged, they are legitimated.

Social change, social criticism, and cultural growth have been largely ineffectual in American society and in the American churches because of the dangerous separation of spirituality and faith from society and justice. Social activists, bereft of the sources of spirit, commitment, lifestyle, and resilient faith, most often fail to bring any total vision or long-haul commitment to social programming and change.

Thus the liberated of one generation become the oppressors in the next. Values are not communicated; the balance of power is. A standard of living is raised; but so is the sense of alienation and depression. For the human spirit has not been touched. And the universe of discourse established by the Commodity Form is never transcended. Social change and institutional restructuring, separated from the life of spirit and faith, lead either to passionless disenchantment or—more frequently—social domination. This domination epitomizes the tragic failure of communism: born of the longings of the human spirit for integrity and joy, communism has matured into a de-spirited and ruthless ideology, pragmatic and manipulative, closed and confining, as demeaning to humanity as the czar or imperialist it had hoped to replace.

On the other hand, when interiorized or ritualized spirituality has isolated itself from the concrete aspirations of oppressed men and women, our dualism has yielded merely passivity and compromise. Acquiescent before injustice, devoid of compassion for fellow human beings, people who have faith without just and loving action are bloodless spirits. And thus, while slaughtered millions are piled upon the altar of history, disincarnate faith dulls its human senses in narcissistic contemplation and self-fulfillment or the formalities of a self-justifying ritual. Men and women, as if in a daze, can continue to approach the Holy Table, breathe in lotus postures, or contribute to collection baskets, while starvation, institutionalized violence and oppression of the poor become the accepted "ways of the world."

If only we Christians might realize the heights to which we are called by our incarnate, covenantal God. If only we might remember the utter newness and brilliance of what our faith implies. No longer would we have to search for some identity, some justification in the garbage heap of commodities. No longer would we clamor for some new savior or seducer. No longer could we even conceive of a fake choice between loving God or loving people, between seeking heaven and building the earth. No longer would we have to rely on some sweet morsel of satisfaction from the year-end *Time* magazine to tell us that our faith is still alive, quivering and groping around for cultural legitimation. In the solitude of prayer's self-presence and the movement of God's Spirit in our hearts, in our standing ontologically naked before our Gospel and Lord, in our mutual sharing of faith and aspiration, we will have discovered not only our God, but our very selves, and other persons as well. And it will be the discovery of the foundations of the only true and permanent revolution.

A revolutionary in the fullest sense of the word—a man or woman who lets the imperative to be human take its deepest hold on his or her being, who becomes wholeheartedly committed to the service of people and a world of justice, who lives as he or she would call others to live—is nothing other than a saint. All of the others—Lenin, Stalin, Maoists, and Weathermen—are imposters. They may have hated Capitalism, but they were themselves variations on its themes of dominance and submission. Francis of Assisi, Loyola, Gandhi, Dorothy Day, Barbara Ward, and E.F. Schumacher are the real revolutionaries. They move people's lives as Christ himself did; they have no time to shift musty furniture. They alone challenge and change the structures of oppression— because they call forth change in the human heart.

A qualitative revolution takes place in the monk who feels with his whole being the total claim that dying to oneself makes upon one's life; it drives him to deeper identification with all humanity, to the service of prayer and simplicity, to the purification of the intolerances within his heart.

Revolution is not in the swinging couple that is "into" liberated sexuality; but it can be found in the man and woman who live a life of sustained committed intimacy and fidelity to each other and their children. Their love and constancy will not only purify themselves and sustain others in their struggles; it will continually lead them outside of themselves into service of community, the transformation of their own style of living, and an abiding confrontation with all the social forms of human impoverishment.

True change is not brought about by the week-end radical or the seasonal rebel or the five-year planner; but it is brought about by the activist whose long-haul commitment radiates with a respect and love for persons. True revolution occurs only when one aspires with the full reach of one's hope to be disengaged from the deadly wheel of the idolized Thing and the violent injustice it necessitates.

It is only the saint who is the true revolutionary. For sanctity is not the quietism of formal rigidity or passionless interiority. Holiness will never occur where there is no passion or zeal for justice. It will never be found where there is no sense of one's own personal poverty nor a corollary love of the poor.

Sanctity is the acceptance of one's humanity, the acknowledgement that one is a loved sinner, and the overflowing of that experience of being unconditionally loved into compassion and honest labor. The saint is not one who displaces old regimes with the latest tyrant or idol. No, the saint does the only utterly new and sacred thing on the face of the earth. The saint has learned to give all—even his or her very self—freely away in a true revolution of life and love.

Saints are all around. One is a pastor to the handicapped who refuses to leave his "little ones" or the poor of his now no longer fashionable neighborhood. One is a judge who has long advocated the rights of the poor and adopted a homeless child as her own. Two of them are a suburban couple who hound supermarkets for unsold food to bring to guests at a Catholic Worker House.

One is a sister without religious garb, working through medical school, praying daily, living in the inner city among the disenfranchised; another is a sister in habit, a hospital administrator, who works for justice at the highest levels of medical leadership while quietly ministering to the poor at each sudden opportunity.

Some revolutionary saints, like Archbishop Romero, Rutilio Grande, and the four U.S. missionaries killed in El Salvador, boldly place their lives in the service of the poor—even at the risk of expulsion, imprisonment, or death. Others, family people, are voluntarily choosing to live poorly so that they may both offer their services to the needy and not be forced to contribute taxation monies for warmaking or any other form of human destruction. Other families, while middle-class economically, are quietly setting limits to their incomes so that their labors and professions are determined by human need and the fruit of their work might be shared with those who have nothing.

A community organizer, living in utter simplicity, developing a spirituality of human failure while he fights to restructure a city's zoning laws is a holy revolutionary. Others are single people living in community, teaching, healing, serving people in their neighborhood, growing in the sacramental life. Still others are retired persons, who yet serve, who contribute silently and anonymously to the building of the earth. Some, finally, have even gone to jail in the name of justice, life, and peace. In each of these concrete human lives there is an interpenetration of faith and history, of God and time, of spirit and society. Each of these lives is revolutionary. Each is holy.

Only when faith and justice are seen as being mutually constitutive, only then is the social and cultural content of spirituality acknowledged and acted upon, only then does the sanctification of human life take place and the saint emerge. Christ only was, only is, when God enters and embraces history. Authentic sanctity, like authentic revolution, is discovered, finally, when human life is seen as so splendid and irreplaceable a value that our very God might become one with it.

Men and women are of inestimable worth, not because they might serve as instruments in generating a gross national product, or even in building the earth, and not because they are capable of production or power and domination, but because in the compassionate embrace of their own truth, in the poverty of their being frighteningly incomplete, they find themselves—vulnerable, yes, but radically opened in freedom to the Fullness of personal knowing and loving. They make incarnate their very God.

Herein alone will we find people of holiness and grace. Herein alone will we find brothers and sisters fully empowered and willing to change the face of the earth.

CHAPTER THIRTEEN

BIBLIOGRAPHICAL APPENDIX

I. THE COMMODITY FORM

A. Psychological, Social, Theoretical Dimensions

1. Henry, Jules. *Culture Against Man* (Vintage, 1965). A strong critique, from the viewpoint of a social-psychologist, of American cultural values. More recent analyses of cultural pretense and mythology include E. Becker's *Denial of Death* (Free Press, 1973), a profound Freudian, religious, and social critique of the "cultural lie," and C. Lasch's *Culture of Narcissism* (Norton, 1978)—again, a Freudian, Marxist, and ethical-religious critique.
2. Key, Wilson Bryan. *Subliminal Seduction* (Signet, 1974). Much data on advertising and the mass media, with their impact—subliminal and overt—on values. See also the earlier works by V. Packard (*Hidden Persuaders* D. McKay, 1957), outdated and not documented and M. McLuhan (*The Mechanical Bride* (Vanguard Press, 1951), highly suggestive and imaginative but, again, outdated, and for the most part elliptical). Key's later books seem a bit paranoid. Other related books include: *The Day the Pigs Refused to be Driven to Market,* by Robin Wight (Random House, 1974);

Open Reality by Richard Altschuler and Nicholas Regush (Putnams, 1974); *The Responsive Chord* by Tony Schwartz (Anchor-Doubleday, 1973); *Assault on Childhood* by Ron Goulart (Sherbourne, 1969); *The Mind Managers* by Herbert I. Schiller (Beacon, 1973).

3. Matson, Floyd. *The Broken Image* (C. Braziller, 1964). A more scientific, philosophical critique of the values underlying the behaviorist-mechanistic human model. This book is both more theoretical and demanding, and at times a bit over-simplified; but it is quite valuable.

4. May, Rollo. *Love and Will* (Norton, 1969), *Man's Search for Himself* (Norton, 1953). Both of these paperbacks, spanning twenty years of reflection by a psychotherapist, probe in a popular manner the meaning of value-loss: in the first instance, with respect to human affectivity, sexuality, and commitment; in the second, with respect to the more foundational purpose and meaning of human life. Other important critical work in this area has been done by Erich Fromm (*The Art of Loving* [Harper and Row, 1956], *Man For Himself* [Rinehard and Co., 1961], *The Revolution of Hope* [Harper and Row, 1968], *The Heart of Man* [Harper and Row, 1964]—all from a psychological, non-believing point of view), by Carl Rogers, and—perhaps most importantly of all—by Abraham Maslow (*Toward a Psychology of Being* [Van Nostrand, 1968]). These are all implicit critiques of our cultural values. From a more religious/psychotherapeutic point of view (quite easy reading) read Viktor Frankl's *Man's Search For Meaning* (Beacon Press, 1963) and *The Doctor and the Soul* (Knopf, 1972), both of which are as inspirational as they are profound.

5. Packard, Vance. *The Status Seekers* (D. McKay, 1959). A popularized, muckraking approach to social differentiation and class analysis.

6. Skinner, B. F. *Beyond Freedom and Dignity* (Knopf, 1971). (Also *Science and Human Behavior* [Free Press, 1965], much more scientific and demanding, and *About Behaviorism* [Vintage, 1976]), the latter's recent popularization.) The first gives a fairly good idea of this man's ideas for our best future. He is immensely powerful in American

psychology, and he represents, in my estimation, the apogee of the Commodity Form as embodied in our behavioral sciences. Skinner's counterpart in biology is Jacques Monod in his *Chance and Necessity* (Knopf, 1971), a book more philosophical and speculative, by a French Nobel scientist.
7. Toffler, Alvin. *Future Shock* (Bantam, 1971). Most have heard about it, many have bought it, but few have read it. It is worth reading, although it is outrageously lacking in any sense of passion, outrage, or moral struggle. Interesting bibliography.

B. Violence

1. The books of Robert Ardrey (*African Genesis* [Collins, 1961]) and Desmond Morris (*Naked Ape* [McGraw Hill, 1967]) are examples of reductionistic, thingified thought in social behavior and zoology with crucial implications for the legitimation of violent behavior, disclaimers notwithstanding.
2. Lionel Rubinoff in *The Pornography of Power* (Quadrangle 1967) and Fredric Wertham in *A Sign for Cain* (Paperback Library, 1969) more ruthlessly and honestly state the dimensions and implications of violent behavior. Cf. E. Fromm's *Anatomy of Human Destructiveness* (Holt, Rinehart and Winston, 1973).

C. Technology

1. Commoner, Barry. *The Closing Circle* (Bantam, 1972). A thoughtful and readable treatment of the ecological crisis and its relation to technology and social impoverishment.
2. Ellul, Jacques. *The Technological Society* (Vintage, 1964). A Christian critique of the technological world and its relationship to values and the putatively legitimate forms of knowledge. Thoroughgoing, heavy, and utterly pessimistic if you are not a Christian of his persuasion.
3. Ferkiss, Victor. *Technological Man* (Mentor, 1969). Ferkiss is at least neutral or positive about technological growth. Strong on data and comprehension, weak on criticism and valuation.

4. Schwartz, Eugene. *Overskill* (Ballantine, 1971). A readable
   and refreshingly pessimistic evaluation of science and its
   knowledge models and products, covering a huge range of
   instances and applications, with a fine bibliography.

D. *Affluence and Empire, Population Jitters, and Special Issues*

1. Domhoff, G. William. *The Higher Circles* (Vintage, 1969).
   This book, with Ferdinand Lundberg's *The Rich and the
   Super Rich* (Bantam, 1968), are heavily documented investigations into the group of families who own and run America.
2. Ehrlich, Paul. *The Population Bomb* (Ballantine, 1971). *The
   End of Affluence* (Ballantine, 1974). Both of these books
   seem to appeal to the worst instincts in men and women.
   They are quite informative on the population problem,
   which is indeed massive, and on the price of consumption-
   expansion, but the answers tend to the metaphysical fall-out
   shelter—abandoning others, holding on to as much as we
   can. *The Doomsday Book* (Fawcett, 1970) by G. R. Taylor
   is equally cautionary but a bit more universalistic, at least to
   the extent that it admits how much we are the cause of the
   problems we face. In the context of population, be sure to
   see the articles listed below.
3. Gailbraith, John Kenneth. *The Affluent Society* (Mentor,
   1958). With the *New Industrial State* (Houghton, Mifflin,
   1971), and his latest book, *Economics and the Public Purpose* (Houghton, Mifflin, 1973), the long-range development and direction of our economy and its relationship to
   values are thoughtfully suggested.
4. Harrington, Michael. *Socialism* (Bantam, 1972). A well-
   written and committed history of socialism, its relationship
   to the humanistic side of Marx, and its possible answers to
   contemporary inequity. Harrington, an ex-Catholic from
   the Mid-West, writes with considerable moral passion—
   sometimes in an oversimplifying manner, but the book is
   quite a fine one. The author has also written the influential
   Other America (Macmillan, 1962), *The Accidental Century*

(Macmillan, 1965) and *Toward a Democratic Left* (Macmillan, 1968).

5. Heilbroner, Robert. *An Inquiry into the Human Prospect* (Norton, 1974). A terribly pessimistic picture of our future in terms of excessive consumption by the wealthy, expenditures on armaments, and the increase in world population. He thinks we could solve the problems (e.g., of world hunger) at hand but that we are and will remain unwilling because of our materialist values. Heilbroner is a foremost economist who has also written the highly readable study of major economic theoreticians (*The Worldly Philosophers* [Simon and Schuster, 1953]) and the best, and one of the most widely used, introductions to economics (*The Economic Problem* [Prentice Hall, 1972]).

6. Mills, C. Wright. *The Power Elite* (Oxford University Press, 1962). One of the earliest (1956) books dealing with the inequities of wealth and the lop-sided lines of political power distributed according to economic power. There is an appeal to latent human values. Philip Slater (*Wealth Addiction* [Dutton, 1980]) and Daniel Bell (*The Cultural Contradictions of Capitalism* [Basic Books, 1976]) offer the most recent analyses of the crisis in values and affect in North American society. These analyses, while in many ways radical, are remarkably conservative in their underlying affirmation of human values.

7. Mitford, Jessica. *Kind and Usual Punishment* (Knopf, 1973). This book, like her previous *American Way of Death,* is an investigative and critical essay on one facet of American cultures and institutions (prisons). It could have been subtitled, "The Commodity Form Behind Bars—Alive and Well."

8. Kubler-Ross, Elizabeth. *On Death and Dying* (Macmillan, 1969). A highly valuable pastoral and critical analysis of how we approach one of life's most fundamental mysteries.

9. Swomeley, John. *American Empire* (Macmillan, 1970). A Christian pacifist unveils the Commodity Form in warmaking. Well documented, intense, and disturbing.

10. Townsend, Claire. *Old Age: The Last Segregation* (Bantam,

1971). A Nader study-group report on nursing homes in this country. Well documented.

Three very valuable articles:

1. "Multinational Corporations: A Reporter at Large," by Richard Barnet and Ronald Muller, *The New Yorker*, Dec. 2, Dec. 9, 1974. Highly articulate, documented, and critical essays on the influence of multinationals on the poor of the world, including our own laboring men and women. Also published in book form, *Global Reach*.
2. "The World Crash" by Geoffrey Barraclough, *N.Y. Review of Books*, Jan. 23, 1975. Total substantiation of Pope Paul's position that world hunger is not most fundamentally a population problem, but an inequity problem. *Highly* valuable.
3. "Triage" by Wade Green, *N.Y. Times Magazine*, Jan. 5, 1975. People not only thinking the unthinkable, but propounding and defending it. Life-boat ethic for the whole world: let the dirty profligate stupid poor die.

II. THE PERSONAL FORM

The papal social teachings (on the dignity of labor, on armaments, peace, and the poor of the Third World) continue to be important reflections on our tradition and its relation to the Commodity Form. See also the documents of Vatican II, the American Catholic Bishops' statements, statements from Latin American Bishops, and the writings of Pope Paul VI and John Paul II. Many of these can be found in *The Gospel of Peace and Justice: Catholic Social Teachings Since Pope John*, presented by Joseph Gremillion (Orbis, 1976).

The foundation is in the Scripture—not only in the prophets, but most especially in the Gospels (Matthew, pre-eminently), which do not suggest a social "gospel" or program, but nonetheless reveal human value, purpose, and salvation as ineluctably opposed to the Commodity Form.

The list below is only a sampling of the variety of approaches to the Personal Form—exemplified in the lives of individuals

(Mother Teresa), in the relationship between faith and justice, and in a Christian-humane approach to economics, war, consumption, and technology.

This bibliography is heavily weighted toward the Catholic tradition—passing over recent valuable work of people like Robert McAfee Brown and other prominent Protestant social theologians and the Inter-religious Task Force for Social Analysis and its fine workbooks in the tradition of radical Protestantism and socialism. In the Jewish tradition, one book which I cannot fail to mention as having enriched my own life is Martin Buber's *I and Thou* (Scribners, 1958).

1. *Poverty in American Democracy.* U.S. Catholic Conference: Campaign for Human Development, November 1974. Can be obtained with the earlier 1972–73 studies on poverty from CHD, 1312 Massachusetts Avenue N.W., Washington DC 20005. A probing and challenging report on justice and its relationship to our professed beliefs as Catholics. Highly valuable, although in some ways statistically dated and theoretically (in terms of economics) incomplete.

2. *Eating as Brothers and Sisters: Meatless Meals and Other Responses to World Hunger.* Institute for the Study of Peace, St. Louis University. A small booklet of meals, practical ideas, and fact sheets. Very good for parish groups.

3. Braaten, Carl. *Christ and Counter Christ* (Fortress, 1972). An interesting, theoretical, somewhat confused treatment of apocalyptic themes in theology and culture. It gets dangerously close to being swallowed up in historicism and unstructured freedom, but it is challenging and imaginative.

4. Brown, Lester. *By Bread Alone* (Praeger, 1974). A thoughtful and meticulous study of the world crisis in population and economic expansion. His spirit is the opposite of Ehrlich and "Triage."

   A more recent analysis of the problem of food distribution, economics, justice, and faith can be found in Jack A. Nelson's *Hunger for Justice* (Orbis, 1980) and the eminently practical and compassionate work by James McGinnis, *Bread and Justice* (Paulist, 1980), which contains a treasure of suggestions, bibliography, and pragmatic wisdom.

5. Day, Dorothy. *Loaves and Fishes* (Harper and Row, 1965), *On Pilgrimage* (Curtis Books, 1972), *The Long Loneliness* (Harper and Row, 1952). All three volumes are worth having. They are diaries, autobiographies, collections of short writings by a woman with a passion for justice and the Gospel of Jesus. A living witness. A fine history of the Catholic Worker movement has been written by W. D. Miller—*A Harsh and Dreadful Love* (Liveright, 1972). See also the works of Jean Vanier, especially *Eruption to Hope* and *Tears of Silence*.

6. Douglass, James W. *The Non-Violent Cross* (Macmillan, 1969), and *Resistance and Contemplation* (Doubleday, 1972). These books are quite moving, quite radical— intelligible, it seems to me, only if Christ is risen.

7. Finnerty, Adam D. *No More Plastic Jesus* (Orbis, 1977) is inspired by the Shakertown Pledge, very issue oriented and at times angry, with much data on injustice—including the wealth of churches in America. *Rich Christians in an Age of Hunger* by Ronald J. Sider (Paulist, 1977) is probably the best in this area; Biblical, religious, data. Good suggestions. *Taking Charge: Personal and Political Change through Simple Living*, by the Simple Living Collective, American Friends' Service Committee (Bantam, 1977). A series of very helpful and imaginatively practical essays on the various areas in our styles of life. Linked to world justice and the Quaker Shakertown Pledge.

8. Freire, Paulo. *Pedagogy of the Oppressed* (Continuum-Seabury, 1970). A Christian-critical approach to education. How the structure itself can embody values both anti-human and counter-Christian.

9. Fritsch, Albert J. *The Contrasumers* (Praeger, 1974). Written by a priest-scientist working with the Center for Science in the Public Interest, this is a very valuable book, crammed with data, brimming with suggestions for personal and group response to conservation and economic simplicity. Contains a "lifestyle index."

10. Goldsen, Rose K. *The Show and Tell Machine* (Delta, 1978). A highly researched study of the contents of television programs. States a strong case against the propagandizing

value-formation of programming, especially in the formation of children's values.

11. Illich, Ivan. *Tools for Conviviality* (Perennial, 1973). A short but penetrating critique of technology-as-end-in-itself. Illich makes far-reaching proposals, although they do not have much concrete embodiment. See also his *Deschooling Society* and *Energy and Equity*.

12. Lewis, C. S. *Mere Christianity* (Macmillan, 1952). Excellent for the moral foundations necessary to perform a cultural critique. Evil is a concrete reality for Lewis (see *That Hideous Strength* [Macmillan, 1946], a science-fiction fantasy novel, *The Great Divorce* [Macmillan, 1946], a parable, *The Abolition of Man* [Macmillan, 1947], a philosophical polemic—all very worthwhile). In *Mere Christianity* he says, "I should not have been honest if I had not told you that three great civilizations had agreed (or so it seems at first sight) in condemning the very thing on which we have [as Christians] based our whole life."

13. Magaña, José. *Strategy for Liberation* (Exposition, 1974). An attempt to relate the Spiritual Exercises of St. Ignatius to social consciousness and political-economic liberation. J. Sobrino's *Christology at the Crossroads* (Orbis, 1978) provides a vision of spirituality that is intensely Christic and social.

14. Mander, Jerry. *Four Arguments for the Elimination of Television* (Morrow, 1978). A wide-ranged critique of television as a form of communication and control. Mander resigned a few years ago as head of one of the most successful advertising companies on the West Coast. He now works on a number of public interest issues. A very challenging and informative book that is attempting to break new ground.

15. Miranda, José. *Marx and the Bible* (Orbis, 1974). Very thorough on the Bible—perhaps *too* thorough—but quite valuable; a mine of texts, especially from the Old Testament. It is not really adequate or critical enough on Marxism. Latin American theologies of liberation are worth looking into, Andrew Greeley notwithstanding. The work of Rubem Alves, Gustavo Gutíerrez, J. Luis Segundo, and work on Dom Helder Camara are increasing in importance. One can

get them all from Maryknoll's Orbis Books, where other fine material—on justice, Third World theology, and the like—can be obtained. Arthur McGovern in *Marxism: An American Christian Perspective* (Orbis, 1980) presents a much needed complement to the work of Miranda. What Miranda does for the scriptural and faith traditions, McGovern does for the Marxian tradition with considerable depth, wisdom, balance, and a remarkable lack of romanticism. His book is much to be recommended to anyone who might hope to integrate the Christian and Marxian traditions.

16. Mische, Gerald and Patricia. *Toward a Human World Order: Beyond the National Security Straightjacket* (Paulist, 1977). Recommended by M. Mead and René Lubos. An imaginative and informative treatment of the crisis in world resources and its effect upon the balance of terror among nations. Strikingly even-handed. An optimistic book, by an author who is convinced we can face our problems and our future with competent organization and a commitment to our religious faith. Recommended highly.

17. Muggeridge, Malcolm. *Something Beautiful for God* (Ballantine, 1973). This little treatment on Mother Teresa needs no comment—just an exhortation to buy it.

18. O'Malley, William. *The Voice of Blood: Five Christian Martyrs of Our Time* (Orbis, 1980). This is a truly uncommon work of integration in the area of spirituality and justice. It is profoundly moving as an account of how five rather ordinary persons embodied the relationship between love and justice in a religious commitment—to such an extent that it required of them the ultimate witness of their lives.

19. Schumacher, E. F. *Small is Beautiful* (Harper, 1974). A well-known British economist, working out of Christian principles and other religious systems, suggests a hard-headed alternative to rampant accumulation and technology. See also his *Guide for the Perplexed* (Harper and Row, 1977) (sound philosophy) and *Good Work* (Harper and Row, 1979).

20. Simon, Arthur. *Bread for the World* (Paulist, 1975). An essential starting point, informed, easy to read, and filled with a sense of justice grounded in Christian faith. It deals

with population, world hunger, lifeboat ethics, environment, poverty in the U.S., foreign aid, armament build-up. Practical suggestions and strong issue orientation.

21. *Sojourners*. A magazine-journal of radical Christian discipleship. A subscription to this publication is most valuable. The publishers live in alternate-style Christian communities. The articles range from prayer and spirituality to racism, disarmament, the prison system, the Third World, multinationals, martyrdom.

22. Taylor, Richard K. *Economics and the Gospel* (United Church, 1973). Well worth having, this little book ties in Scripture and social consciousness in a simple and clear way. Good bibliography, footnotes, study questions, and research. I highly recommend this book—even though it does not really probe the practical economic implications of massively employed Christian principles.

23. Ward, Barbara, with René Dubos. *Only One Earth* (Ballantine, 1972). A compassionate and thoughtful study of the population-technology matrix by two great humanist believers—Lady Jackson (Barbara Ward), a brilliant economist and Dubos, a renowned scientist and writer. Ward, with Mother Teresa, is one of the greatest Christians alive; and all of them point to the living diversity of how we might embody faith as well as a passion for justice.

24. Winn, Marie. *The Plug-In Drug: Television, Children, and the Family* (Viking, 1977). A very important contribution concerning the effects of television on our culture as a whole, especially in relation to the formation of values and consciousness in the young. Winn deals not merely with the content of television programs, but also with the very form and act of watching television during the crucial stages of early childhood development. It contains much data, a lot of first-hand testimony, many practical suggestions, and a penetrating discussion of the relationships between television and the development of the brain, the activity of reading, the decline in logic, loss of creativity, incidents of hyperactivity and violence, passivity, decline of the family, the decline of play, the decline of commitment.